ALSO BY EILEEN K. WADE

*The Piper of Pax*
*Twenty-one Years of Scouting*
*The Boys' Life of the Chief Scout*
*Twenty-seven Years with Baden-Powell*

# Contents

# *Illustrations*

**A***

*My dear Guides,*

*And I include Seniors and Brownies and Guiders and all of you, and the Scout people too—everyone in fact who is bound by the Promise and Law of our Movement.*

*There was a time when I could have spoken to each one of you individually and given you a left-handshake, as I do to a great many of you every week—but as our family now numbers not hundreds of thousands but millions, and is so widely scattered about the world, I just can't get round to you all.*

*So here is the next best thing—a book through which I hope you will not only get to know* ME *more as a person, but also will get to know what I think and feel about* YOU, *and how deeply I care for every single one of you, whoever and wherever you may be.*

*Olave Baden-Powell*

# I

# *A Perch in a Palace*

LET me introduce you to the World Chief Guide, not, at first, amongst thousands of Guides at a Rally, but in her own lovely home.

Alongside the River Thames, not many miles from London, stands the romantic Palace of Hampton Court, the home and headquarters for many years of the Kings and Queens of England and their Courts.

Here history takes a long walk from the pages of printed books and comes to life among the actual haunts of storied monarchs. There you may walk along Tennis Court Lane to the court where the old game—the father of our lawn tennis—was played, and indeed is still played by a few people; here you may see the bunches of grapes ripening on the Black Hamburg vine, planted during the reign of King

George III. This vine has been known to bear more than two thousand bunches of grapes in one year.

Here you may see the first Queen Elizabeth's windows, with her initials and the date 1568 carved beneath each; and here also you might have seen the second Queen Elizabeth at a great Ball in the year of her Coronation.

Here you may walk through the unhappy Anne Boleyn's gateway, above which the immense clock, presented to the Palace by King William IV, chimes out the hours, half-hours, and quarters.

And here too you may find the Chief Guide today.

The first King to live at Hampton Court Palace was that much-married monarch Henry VIII. It had been the home of Cardinal Wolsey who, you may remember, had a difference of opinion with the King on a question of divorce. In the hope of regaining the King's lost favour, the Cardinal handed over his beautiful home, lock, stock, and barrel, as a gift.

The last King to use Hampton Court as a royal residence was George II. Later it became the home of many different people. Suites of rooms, known as 'Grace and Favour' apartments, were allotted by the reigning monarch to the widows or children of distinguished servicemen or statesmen—those who had given outstanding service to their country. Sometimes the distinguished men themselves ended their lives there, as in the case of Field Marshals Wolseley and Birdwood; but for the most part the occupants are ladies.

It was not surprising, therefore, that when the Founder and Chief of our great Scout and Guide Movement died in Kenya in 1941, one of these 'Grace and Favour' apartments was at once offered to his widow, to be a rent-free home for the rest of her life. It was a mark of the nation's gratitude.

That then, in brief, is an account of how Olave, Lady Baden-Powell came to live at Hampton Court and make her home in the Palace.

I have called it a home, but actually perhaps it is more of a 'perch' where she rests between long flights and to which she returns for brief intervals in her busy life.

She has other perches too: one in Kenya, which was her last home with the Founder, and to which she loves to return whenever she gets a chance; one at 'Our Chalet' in Switzerland; another at 'Our Cabaña' in Mexico; another at Foxlease in England; and indeed one could go on for a long time listing the 'Guide Houses' about the world where a bed and a welcome are always awaiting her. I will tell you more about them in a later chapter. But Hampton Court Palace is her permanent address in England for as long as she likes to live there.

Close by is London Airport, and it is from there that the World Chief Guide takes off on her many flights abroad; and it is to London Airport that, her mission accomplished, she returns on her homing flight, often late in the evening. From Canada or the U.S.A., from Iceland, Switzerland, Germany, and many another country, she comes flying in to rest in her peaceful old Palace for a few days or weeks before starting out on yet another journey.

Lady Baden-Powell's apartment is in the Tudor part of the Palace and is approached by Tennis Court Lane or the Master Carpenter's Court—romantic names bringing before the mind's eye some of the Palace's earlier inhabitants.

In her large bedroom, with its turret 'powder closet' adjoining, William Shakespeare is said to have worked out some of his plays which were certainly acted in the Great Hall just below. From the old windows of her long corridor one looks out on the great West gateway through which streams of visitors pass daily on their tour of the Palace.

Up here all is quiet and, except for the striking of the clock, not a sound penetrates the thick walls and one feels completely isolated from the crowds of people below.

Linking the Chief Guide's main apartment with her 'annexe' is a delightful little roof-garden, bright in spring with wallflowers and tulips and in summer with scarlet geraniums. Here she is often to be found at tea-time, either enjoying a few minutes' quiet relaxation from her typewriter or, more probably, talking to the visitors who come to see her from every corner of the free world. These visitors vary in size and shape and age, in colour, creed, and career, and in many other ways. But one thing they nearly always have in common:

*'They are Guides, all Guides,*
 *And in unexpected places you will meet their friendly faces*
 *And a ready hand besides;*
 *And there's not much danger of finding you're a stranger*
 *For Commissioner or Ranger,*
 *They are Guides, all Guides.'*

Sometimes it may be a party of Eclaireuses from France, or of green-uniformed Girl Scouts from the United States; or Japanese or Indians in their bright robes; or mere Britishers from Commonwealth Headquarters. Hampton Court Palace is on the itinerary of almost every tourist from overseas, and amongst every party of these there are bound to be Guides or Scouts or leaders of the Movement whose one ambition is to shake hands—left hands—with their Chief.

On the roof-garden they will eat buns and drink fruit squash or tea, provided by what the Chief Guide calls her 'Home Office Staff'—as distinct from the World Bureau Staff and Commonwealth Headquarters Staff in London.

For a time the talk will be general. She will ask them many questions about their home Guiding, and about her friends in that particular part of the world, their adventures on tour, their hobbies and interests, and so on. Then there will be an expectant pause.

Tea has been cleared away and the visitors will arrange themselves to listen quietly while the Chief Guide gives them a little talk, telling of her own adventures in her latest trips abroad, and reminding them that as 'ambassadors of friendship' they too can carry out a valuable service for their Movement and, ultimately, for the peace of the world; because Guides who have worked and played and sung and prayed together at camp-fires under the stars, and visited one another's home countries, will have no wish to snatch from one another or to quarrel in the years to come.

When the tea and the talk is over and the photography too—for very many of the visitors have their cameras at the ready—a move is made indoors. There they will spend another hour or so looking round the apartment, admiring the Founder's many trophies, his caskets and swords of honour, his water-colour sketches which adorn every wall, and—above all—the dozens of scrapbooks which contain mementos of his and the Chief Guide's travels in many lands. There are more than fifty of these volumes, containing a pictorial history of Scouting and Guiding. Each visitor will turn first to the pages referring to her own country, delighted to read the cuttings and look at the photographs and sketches of friends and familiar places. Some of the Founder's most charming water-colour sketches are to be found in these scrapbooks, the making of which has been Lady Baden-Powell's spare-time hobby through the years.

At last, with handshakes and grateful farewells, the visitors will stage a reluctant departure and take themselves off to admire the State rooms or formal gardens of the Palace. But, judging by the letters that come pouring in afterwards, the high-light of it all has been this intimate visit to the home of their Chief Guide. Her enthusiastic welcome and undoubted interest in what they are doing, no less than her quiet words, will have inspired hundreds of girls to make their Guide life a more real contribution towards the attainment of the peace and goodwill for which we so often pray.

During the 1953 Coronation year, when the whole

Guide Movement throughout the Commonwealth carried out special good turns as a 'Coronation Tribute' to their young Queen, so lately herself a Patrol Leader, the Chief Guide thought out a tribute all of her own. This was to furnish, camp fashion, some of the empty rooms in her 'annexe' across the roof, so that Guiders and Guides coming to England for the Coronation might find somewhere to stay within easy reach of overcrowded London and the Coronation route. Nearly three hundred Guide folk, in relays, enjoyed this privilege of staying with their Chief while sharing in the fun of Coronation Year; and the immense trouble which the Chief Guide, and her friend and helper, Miss Rust, took in arranging for their comfort and happiness will long be remembered in many lands. Although she herself saw the Coronation from a privileged position, I think the Chief Guide's far greater happiness was derived from the fact that she had enabled so many others to have a chance of being there. For she is a born 'sharer'.

One of the Founder's mottoes for the Guides was illustrated by him in a drawing of a signpost, with the wording: '*Turn to the right and keep straight on.*' That would still be his wish for every member of his Movement.

But there are many good paths to the right and not every one leads to a palace. In the next few chapters

I am going to show you how quite an ordinary girl—not so particularly different from you or me—came to be the loved leader of millions of girls scattered about the world and thus to achieve real greatness.

# 2

# A Child in Chesterfield

'And Nature, the old Nurse, took
The child upon her knee'

FEBRUARY 22ND ('Thinking Day') was the birthday
both of the Founder of Scouting in 1857 and—thirty-
two years later—of his wife.

In the Founder's lifetime someone suggested—at a
World Conference in Poland—that this should be
kept each year as a special day when Guides everywhere would think of one another and exchange
greetings. With each year that has passed, the day has
become more widely recognized as a time when
Guides and Girl Scouts not only send greetings to
each other and to their Chief, but when they also
contribute their pennies to a fund for helping their
more needy sisters.

On Thinking Day if she happens to be in England

Lady Baden-Powell is completely snowed under—indoors if not out. There are letters, messages, cables, telegrams, packages, parcels, and greetings of every kind.

This day has been spent by the Chief Guide in very many different parts of the world—seldom in the same place for two successive years—but always with Guides in some part of her domain.

Before we look at her birthday post let me take you back to a Thinking Day of long ago, before most of you people were even thought of, let alone doing your own thinking!

I have chosen it at random from the Chief Guide's diary of February 22nd, 1936.

With the Founder she was in South Africa, in the town of Pietermaritzburg, the capital of the Province of Natal (now part of the Union of South Africa).

A huge Scout and Guide Rally had been arranged in their honour, and the day started in hot sunshine, with telegrams pouring in from every part of the world to prove that Guides everywhere were with them in thought, even though they could not be there in person to join in the fun.

Pietermaritzburg is a bright, cheerful little town, with lovely views of distant mountains, and on its outskirts a fine residential centre with nice houses and gardens ablaze with beautiful flowers—yes, in February!

But as the day went on clouds appeared in the sky and by the time the Scouts and Guides had mustered at the Rally ground, two miles out of the town, the rain had come down in torrents and driven the whole lot scurrying back to the Town Hall for the birthday party. There was an immense birthday cake—'like a pantechnicon'—and all ended happily because Scouts and Guides are not daunted by mere weather; but the Founder certainly had a reputation for bringing down the rain on a Rally or Jamboree.

In some places he came to be known as 'The Rain-maker'; but of course he always said that he did it on purpose, just to see what stuff the Scouts and Guides were made of. It is easy enough to smile and look happy on a sunny day, but it takes a good stiff upper lip to keep the smile fixed when the rain is pouring down and the once smart uniform has become sodden and dripping. On that particular day the African Wayfarers and Sunbeams (their names for Guides and Brownies) had the best of it, for they had their big Rally in the morning when the sun was shining and were able to give their displays out of doors, and the Chief Guide was thrilled with all that she saw.

*'Kind thoughts are certainly circling the earth today,'* she

wrote, '*and we ourselves feel quite overwhelmed by the kindliness showered upon us in thought from afar and greetings from those around us. All that we can say is Thank You, Thank You, Thank You.*'

But from the sunny South Africa of those days we must now return to that Palace in England and see some of the messages that the postman has brought in a special great sack.

Here is one from the Girl Guides of Korea—and written in beautiful English. Next to it is a message from Egypt: then Brazil and Chile, Holland and Portugal, Kenya, Uganda, Tanganyika—not just one message from each country but scores of little individual letters as well. The greetings cards are often home-made and beautifully designed, and these come from companies, troops, and individual Scouts and Guides in every place where they exist to send them. Each message, as she opens the envelope, takes the Chief Guide back in thought to the last day that she spent with those particular members of her family.

'*Iceland!*' she will exclaim. '*Dear little people. That was where we climbed the mountain that evening and had our camp-fire. How it all comes back to me!*'

Then perhaps Mexico. '*I can see them all in my mind's eye at the Cabaña on that lovely day I spent there!*'

'*New Zealand—that's where the great Think will have*

*begun.*' For in New Zealand each year the Guides climb a mountain to see the sun rise—its earliest rising time—and there they have their little ceremony of prayer and thought which starts the ball rolling.

And so on through the pile, each one bringing to mind some joyous occasion, a Rally or a camp-fire or just a cosy evening chatting in some fellow-Guide's home. Memories come flooding back bringing their happiness with them.

Each message is gratefully acknowledged. To the Chief Guide, as to the Founder of Scouting, '*nothing is yours until you have said thank you for it*'; and this applies not only to life and home and health and happiness and all God's other gifts but also to letters and presents. This means quite a lot of extra work for an already busy person, but it is happy work, bringing in its train so many assurances of love and friendship.

Here is a heavy parcel. Whatever can be inside it? A Pack of Brownies in Edinburgh have been having a Thinking Day party; and each Brownie has polished up a penny until it shines like the sun—on both sides. Then Brown Owl has fastened all the pennies on to a stout piece of cardboard and sent them to the Chief Guide, to be given to the Thinking Day fund. What fun it must have been, seeing whose penny shone the brightest; what fun to join in giving this birthday present; and what fun for the Chief Guide to get it.

And, incidentally, what good practice for polishing up Brownie badges.

Another parcel contains something a bit sticky. '*We had our Thinking Day party early because we thought we would like to send you some of our cake to eat on your birthday.*' And so it goes on—all day and for several days—thinking and thanking.

Hullo! Here is something from Chesterfield in Derbyshire. The Chief Guide lingers over this message and looking out of the window she sees with her mind's eye not the frosty earth outside but the green fields on which she looked from her nursery window.

Chesterfield was once a Roman station on the road from Derby to York.

Since the thirteenth century it has been mainly famous for the unusual twisted spire on its church—due to the action of the sun upon the lead, warping the insufficiently seasoned timbers.

A more fanciful legend is that the Devil, passing over Chesterfield in one of his flights, perched on the spire not knowing that it belonged to a church. Service was in progress, and the incense, ascending, irritated the diabolical nose so that he sneezed violently, causing the spire to contract before he could remove his tail from around it.

But the Devil's name is not the only one that has

been associated with Chesterfield. Good people have
helped to make its history. It was the last resting place
of George Stephenson, the famous engineer. His still
more famous son, Robert, was the godfather of the
Founder of the Boy Scouts and provided him with his
first two names—Robert Stephenson.

Chesterfield will have yet another claim to fame in
years to come—as the birthplace of the Chief Guide.

Stubbing Court, where Olave St. Clair Soames was
born in 1889, was a large Georgian house, five miles
west of the town. As the youngest of a little family of
three, Olave received a very warm welcome and was
everybody's darling.

Her father, Harold Soames, was the manager of a
large brewery business which he had inherited from
his father, and he had to go in to his office every day,
riding or walking the five miles. Although he made a
success of the business and was able to retire while
still quite young, he was not by choice a business man
but an artist to his fingertips. Architecture, scenery,
and painting were his great interests and he was himself a good water-colourist.

Olave remembers nothing of Stubbing Court, for
she was only a year old when a move was made to
West House, nearer to the town. Here she spent many
hours with nose pressed against the nursery window,
looking out on a field where horse fairs were held.

She loved horses and also remembers delightful visits to the stables after church on Sundays, to watch the fine brewery horses enjoying their day of rest.

The house was an attractive one of red brick with an old-world garden behind high walls—an ideal place for children—and not too far from the shops and office.

Here then we can picture the Chief Guide, a tiny little dark-haired elf, spending her happy and un-eventful babyhood, with devoted parents, a friendly older brother and sister, and a succession of nurses and nursery governesses, both French and English.

Olave was only four when Miss Wilson, their first real governess, joined the family. Arthur and Auriol now began regular lessons and Olave joined them for walks with 'Wissie', as they called her, and delighted in the stories which she was always ready to tell them.

The three children, and Olave especially, loved all living creatures, whether horses or dogs, doves or baby chickens. Many years later she wrote in *The Guide*:

'*As a child I was rather frightened of grown-ups. They seemed so different somehow and didn't love rabbits and doves as I did. They just called them "animals" and "birds" and didn't want to hold them and hug them as I did.*'

A very deep love, whether for animals or human beings, is not all happiness. Olave shed many tears in those days for her pets, and felt deeply the loss of a favourite animal. She has never lost this love for animals and whether writing of her doves in those long-ago days, her dogs at Pax Hill, or her pet hyrax in Kenya, she used just the same terms of endearment. '*A Guide is a friend to animals*' and this was certainly true of the Chief Guide from her very earliest days.

It was in her third beautiful Derbyshire home, Renishaw Hall, which her father rented from the Sitwell family, that Olave's education began in earnest. Friede, a young German governess, here came on the scene and became the lifelong friend of the whole family.

Renishaw Hall was perhaps the most stately of her homes. It had belonged to the Sitwells since Cromwellian times and has been fully described in many of Osbert Sitwell's books. His father, Sir George Sitwell, was rather like Harold Soames in wishing to be on the move in search of fresh beauty in nature or architecture; and for months on end he took his own family to one of his other houses and let Renishaw. The house is a veritable museum of lovely and priceless furniture, pictures, and hangings. But Olave was not of an age to appreciate famous tapestries and her memories are of animals and particularly of three cart-horses which walked into the hall one day and caused quite a stir in the household.

At Renishaw, with her father and mother and brother and sister, Olave spent happy days, getting into the usual childish scrapes and mischief, learning her lessons, and suffering the drawbacks, as well as enjoying the privileges, of being the youngest.

She was learning to knit and had made a 'comforter' as a present for one of the keepers on the estate. She was seven years old at this time and her hair was cut short like a boy's.

Proud of her handiwork, she carried it out and formally presented it to the old gentleman.

'And what did he say?' asked her mother.

'Oh, he said "Thank you, my little man," ' said Olave.

'And what did you say to that?'

'Well,' replied Olave grandly, 'I didn't undeceive him as I thought it might hurt his feelings.'

An early instance of what we all notice about the Chief Guide today: her constant thought for the feelings of the person who reads a letter or hears a remark.

A less happy event at Renishaw was when Olave fell over the banisters on to a skylight and would most certainly have been killed but for the prompt action of her older sister. But she was quite badly hurt and for a long time afterwards had to be specially watched and cared for. Her cheeks, once so rosy, became pale and wan.

Brother Arthur had gone away to school when the family moved again, this time to Bryerswood, a charming house with a wonderful view overlooking the lake at Windermere.

Here, with her sister and Friede, Olave recovered her strength. She led a real 'Guide-y' life in the open air and throve on it.

The three of them would take their lesson books and their lunch out on to the moors, even in winter, and after a morning's work would have their picnic meal and then go for a long walk or learn to sing folk-songs out in the fresh, clean lakeland air.

Happy, carefree days!

Looking back down the years, the World Chief Guide feels that she was perhaps spoilt and that this haphazard education did not give her the best chances for making good.

But education is best judged by its results.

Olave never went to school, even for a day. Her father and mother did not want her to be forced into a mould and turned out just like everybody else.

She did not care very much for books, but loved music and learned to appreciate the best. Her free life in the open air in those early days probably gave her that stamina which has enabled her in later life to stand up to overwork, to play her part in all weathers at Guide Rallies, to sit in damp surroundings at camp-fires, and to fulfil months on end of speaking engagements during repeated tours year after year, with hardly a day off for illness or a date cancelled.

And she learned a great deal about the natural world. Her freedom to revel in the open air and to devote herself to animals and birds encouraged in her that love and sympathy for all God's creatures which school books can never supply.

Neither of Olave's parents had achieved worldly fame, though both were possessed of many talents and graces. But they were good and happy people. They lived a quiet dignified life, in reasonably easy circumstances, preferring the country to the town. Their days were busy with their own artistic and domestic pursuits and with the careful upbringing of their three children.

So, although Olave was not exactly born to greatness, she had as good a chance as most people of making a success of her life—if she made the most of her opportunities.

B

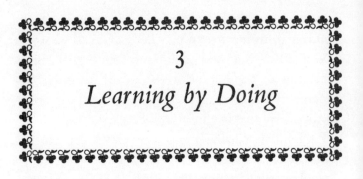

# 3
# *Learning by Doing*

IF I were to say to you that Olave Baden-Powell, the Chief Guide, is a unique person (and how many people do say it!) I should not really be telling you anything remarkable, because you and I—and everyone else in the world—are unique too.

'Unique' means 'the only one of its kind'.

The remarkable thing would be if we found two people who were exactly alike.

Has it ever occurred to you how true that is? Take outward appearance only. Of all the millions of people in the world there is no one exactly like you, in face, form, or feature. To me it has always seemed positively amazing that with two eyes, a nose, and a mouth, and an identical number of arms, legs, bones, and muscles, each person born into the world is yet completely different—a new design from the mind of God the Creator.

Your family and your friends may be near and dear to you. They may even be a bit like you, but they are not *you*. You are a separate being, entirely on your own. However much you may try to look like somebody else you will never succeed because you are meant to be yourself.

It is the same with your mind and your soul. No one ever dreams the dreams that you dream or thinks exactly the same thoughts. You have a niche in the world to fill which has been made for no one else, and it is up to you to find it and to fit yourself into it. Your ideas, your special abilities, talents, and tastes are there for you to develop and make the best use of.

That is one way in which the Guide Movement, with its badge system, comes in useful. You go in for some particular badge not just because you want another decoration on your arm, or because you are necessarily going to do embroidery or keep bees for a living, but because by choosing what badge you want to work for you are finding out what sort of person you are and where your tastes and abilities lie. This knowledge will be of value when you do come to choose your career.

And how much better to be the person that you

were meant to be, and to do the job that you were meant to do, than to be a feeble copy of someone else!

So, instead of saying that the Chief Guide is unique, I will put it like this: she is a person who has always recognized and appreciated her uniqueness. She has never tried to make herself exactly like any other girl or woman, and, instead of envying other people's gifts or opportunities, she has made the fullest use of her own.

Perhaps the fact that she never went to school helped her in this. At school it is very easy just to become one of a crowd, and to want things merely because the others want them or have them.

The Chief Guide has never done or wanted anything for those reasons. She has always done things either because she thought them right or because she thought them enjoyable—and there are really no other good reasons for doing anything.

Yet how many of us waste time by pretending to enjoy things which don't really appeal to us at all, just because we don't want to be left out. Some of us go further and even do what we know to be wrong because we don't dare to be different. We forget that we are human beings and unique; instead we behave more like woolly sheep.

Because of being herself, the Chief Guide gets satisfaction or enjoyment or both out of everything she does. It may be Guiding or travelling or home-making, or seeing a good play or film, or making a scrapbook or entertaining her friends. She does not play bridge or go to many cocktail parties, not because she thinks these entertainments wrong but because she does not enjoy them. She does not colour her lips or her fingernails or have her hair permanently waved. Nor does she feel it necessary to wear unbecoming clothes just because they are fashionable. She is content to be herself and to judge for herself. She is a leader, not a follower.

Perhaps the education which she received at home helped in this. Living a great deal with grown-ups and listening to their conversation without being expected to join in it, the child Olave got into the way of thinking matters out for herself. She still does this and never takes for granted that what she reads in newspapers and books is necessarily true. She likes to know both sides of a case before deciding on its merits.

Through living with cultured and intelligent people she also learned to appreciate the best, whether in music, literature, or art.

Not long ago, when travelling in the United States, Lady Baden-Powell was staying in a friend's house.

Americans are very quick to appreciate beauty in ancient buildings. In America anything that has stood for more than a hundred years is regarded as old and therefore of great interest. When Americans come to England they are intensely interested in our ancient buildings. This friend had quite a picture gallery in her hall, showing some of the 'stately homes of England'.

On being shown these pictures the Chief Guide had to admit that, though by no means a millionaire, she had at one time or another lived in many of these houses. In his search for beauty for himself and his family her father was always on the look-out for lovely places which could be rented for short periods. This explains why, up to the time of her marriage, Olave had lived in some seventeen different homes.

And even now, at Hampton Court Palace, she is following in her father's footsteps by residing in what is perhaps the most stately home of all.

In 1898, when Olave was nine, her father decided that he had had enough of the bleak north. He took a house in St. James's Place, London, for his family, while he himself went abroad to paint. But London did not suit Olave. She developed diphtheria and whooping-cough in rapid succession and pined for the free life and fresh air of the countryside. A temporary home was found at Pixton Park, near Dulverton, on the borders of Devon and Somerset. It meant a lot to this child to be in the country once more and to be able to have her animals around her and to keep hens. This had been her sixth home in nine short years and it must have seemed a normal part of existence to Olave to be packing and unpacking her treasures and settling her pets into their new surroundings.

Perhaps that is why today she is the best of home-makers, finding it worth while to make a place comfortable and homely even if it is only for a mere night or two in camp. Any overnight visitors to her home are always tremendously impressed by the thoughtful comforts and warm welcome she provides.

It was at Cranborne Manor, in Dorset, a year later, that poultry-keeping became a real business concern in the hands of Olave and her sister and their governess.

'*April 15th, 1900*', says the diary of this eleven-year-old: '*All to church. Pulley, our dear darling black langsham hen had six babies. We had her at Pixton in 1898 and we love her. She sits in the swing with us. All the hens and chickens belong to Auriol and me and we sell eggs, etc. to Mother. It is called the C.P.F., "Cranborne Poultry Farm".*'

Of her many homes Cranborne was perhaps in some ways the most beautiful. Dating from the time of Athelstane it had been a hunting box of King John when he pursued the wily deer on Cranborne Chase early in the thirteenth century. The house belongs to Lord Salisbury and, within easy reach of Foxlease, is worth a visit by Guides.

At Cranborne, with its wonderful old garden and smooth lawns, its bowling alley, tennis and croquet grounds, Olave first began to take an interest in organized games. She learned to play tennis under her father's instruction, and also to ride on her pony, Peggy. She confided to her diary that '*I fell off lots of times but these things aren't mentioned*'.

Although she did not go to school, Olave worked fairly strenuously at that time at her lessons at home, judging by another entry in the famous diary:

'*June 12th, 1900. Usual lessons. Begin at 8. Auriol practises the piano. I do, on Mondays and Thursdays, History, on Tuesdays and Fridays, Geography, on Wednesdays and Saturdays, sums, which I positively loathe. Breakfast at 9. Walk from 10–11. Lessons from 11–1. Lunch. Lessons again from 2–4. Tea 4.30. Dinner at 7. C'est tout. We have a half-holiday every Saturday and do the flowers violently in the schoolroom to look nice for Sunday.*'

'Learning by Doing' is what I have called this chapter, and it is what the Founder and the Chief Guide have always believed in and practised.

The sums, so 'positively loathed' when they came into the before-breakfast lesson hour, were quite pleasant when performed as 'accounts rendered' by the Cranborne Poultry Farm for eggs supplied to the house. It is always so much easier to learn things when one sees the necessity for them, and in keeping her egg records and adding up her bills Olave learned to enjoy working at this hitherto hated subject.

It was at Cranborne, in the winter before her eleventh birthday, that Olave began to keep this diary, from which I have quoted, of her day-to-day adventures. Ever since that time she has kept it up with the greatest regularity.

I wonder if you have ever begun to keep a diary, urged on by a Christmas present of a tempting little leather-covered book? Such booklets have a way of being filled up most meticulously all through January and half of February, less regularly through March, and, alas, from April onwards the pages often remain blank.

The fact that Olave did not treat her diary in this casual manner speaks volumes—the right word there —for the fact that even at eleven years old she had a bit of what the Founder used to call 'stickability'. Little did she think, as she filled in the pages in a laborious hand, that in the years to come this story of her early life would be of interest to thousands of people in addition to her own children and grandchildren for whose benefit alone they were written.

In later life the Chief Guide has had to do a great deal of writing, and not only in her diary. She has had to write many books and articles and stories, and, though she still maintains that she finds writing difficult, she has an original way of expressing herself so that people always enjoy reading what she has written. It was partly from her diary writing, and partly from her mother's example, that she gained the ability to put her thoughts into words.

Mrs. Soames had written her own life story, not for publication, but for her own children to read and treasure. Each of them was given a copy of it in order that they might know more about their mother and perhaps learn from her experience how to live happy lives.

'*It will help you*', she wrote, '*to think sometimes of one who loved you so dearly. It will help you to remember her whose most earnest wish was to teach you to become, in the highest sense, acceptable to the world—and so acceptable to God.'*

It was a happy idea and one which brought inspiration and encouragement to her children.

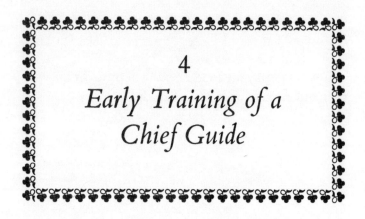

# 4

# *Early Training of a Chief Guide*

IF SHE had known that she would one day be called upon to be the World Chief Guide how do you suppose Olave Soames would have trained herself for the job?

Would she have tried to get all the badges in every possible subject and the highest Guide qualifications in the way of cords and diplomas?

Or would she have specialized in learning foreign languages?

No one could really answer that question because when she was a girl there were no such things as Guides and no idea that there ever would be. There were not even any Boy Scouts at the time of which I write.

Olave would no doubt have been a very keen Brownie if there had been Brownie Packs, because, as we read her diary, we realize more and more how she loved doing things—just as all Brownies do. Whether it was washing up or riding, or helping to unpack the china or nursing sick pets, or learning to sing and to play the violin, she always enjoyed the active doing of a thing so much more than reading about how it should be done. She was very active on her feet and never walked if she could run!

The Chief Guide is much the same today. After long hours of work at her desk she loves nothing better than to get hold of a fork or a spade and dig ferociously in her garden. No weeds have much chance of survival when she is around, for '*I do like to do it thoroughly while I am at it*' is one of her watch-words—and this, of course, is the watchword also of every true Guide.

When of Brownie age, Olave went to classes in Bournemouth for dancing and gymnastics. Brownies will sympathize with her when she told her diary that she had been catching balls and skipping but '*I can't yet do doubles at skipping*'. Doubtless this matter was soon put right, for Olave was always a great trier.

It is, of course, just possible that she might have embarked on her career as a Chief Guide with more confidence if she had had some specialized training, such as present-day Guiders are lucky enough to get at Foxlease and elsewhere, but I don't think, do you, that it could have made her into a better Chief Guide?

After all, Scouting and Guiding is not a complicated science. It is a simple scheme, in the form of a game, for helping people to get the most out of their lives; to prove that character and health matter more than money and possessions; that the truest happiness comes from caring for and serving other people; and that friendship is one of the finest things in the world.

Scouting and Guiding may perhaps be compared to a large pie into which the Founder put all the best ingredients in life and for which he gave us the recipe. He did not make the ingredients but he did invent the mixture, test it, and find that it made a good pie, and then write down the recipe. It is this mixture that has helped so many boys and girls, and grown-ups too, to achieve happiness during the last fifty years.

Other people have thought out mixtures and made pies which have not always been so well balanced. Most of these pies have contained good ingredients, but in some cases the makers have left out religion— and our Founder knew that no one could live a full or happy life without God. Others have left out fresh air and exercise and so have turned people into pallid students; others again have concentrated on health, beauty, or fashion, and have forgotten to sweeten the mixture with good turns and thoughtfulness for others. So their pies have not kept well.

The Founder's pie—Scouting and Guiding—contains the ingredients which all really good, happy, and successful people in the world have known about and used, whether or not they called themselves Scouts and Guides. They have known how to use things in their proper proportions—and that is the secret of a good mixture.

When you have read more about Lady Baden-Powell you will agree that she was getting to know this long before she could call herself a Guide—when she was just Olave Soames living at home with her parents.

From her childhood she seems to have realized that life had been given her to be used and not wasted; that she owed God some 'rent' in the way of service, and that He meant us to enjoy our time on the earth and to make the most of it.

At home she was able to learn and practise many of the things now included in the Guide Promise and Law—duty to God and the practice of good turns, courtesy, obedience, loyalty, friendship, and kindness to animals; and in these ways she was unwittingly training herself for the future.

When she was twelve years old Olave paid her

first visit to France, and this was the beginning of the travels abroad which in later years have been so much a part of her Guide life.

Away from her beloved home pets, she made friends with the sturdy little donkeys which carried the family on their backs for whole-day expeditions up the steep mountainsides, climbing through olive orchards and orange groves, up the narrow stone trackways sloping at steep angles and often terraced in shallow steps.

How much this visit must have come back to her when fifty years later she visited a Guide camp at Les Courmettes, that lovely Guide house of modern times, set high on a mountain plateau, nearly three thousand feet above the Mediterranean.

This camping centre was given to the Fédération Français des Eclaireuses in 1939, and since then many hundreds of Guides of many countries have helped to develop the sixteen hundred acres of land. Every Guider, Ranger, or Guide who goes to Les Courmettes takes her share in the work, either in pulling up brambles, breaking up the soil, wood-cutting, working in the garden, haymaking, or harvesting, as well as helping in the house.

There are many difficulties to be faced when living on a mountain-top, but those tough Guides who find their way to the summit discover the climb well

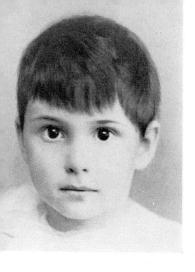

*Olave St. Clair Soames, aged three*

*A happy family at Pax Hill, Bentley, 1926*

The Americans call them 'Girl Scouts' but they are all part of the same family—and a very large part. They celebrated their Golden Jubilee in 1962

Their World Chief greets Girl Scouts at a camp in the mountains in California

worth while. The ascent, with mules laden with camp equipment, is picturesque but rough going. It is no small matter to bring to the mountain-top tents, packs, and campers, by a zig-zag track which has twenty-nine turns in it.

But the Chief Guide, in 1954, made this ascent, in order to join fifteen hundred Guides who were carrying out what they called 'L'Expédition 1954', and she enjoyed it as much as any of them.

More than fifty years earlier, when Olave had made that first journey to the South of France, there were no motor-cars for touring round in. There are plenty of cars today, but it is still 'Shanks's mare'—or a tough little donkey or mule—if you want to climb that mountain.

It was at about this time that Olave began her violin lessons and she enjoyed these very much. Her father had given her a good violin and good masters to teach her; and she kept up her 'fiddling' until her more onerous duties as Chief Guide made it impossible to find the necessary time for practice. Then, instead of allowing her beautiful fiddle, named 'Diana', to lie idle, she handed it to the British Girl Guides for competition among the musical members.

At the age of twelve and a half—very much earlier than most people leave school, and at a time when

some girls are just going to their first boarding-school
—Olave's education was pronounced by her parents
to be complete. When I say education I mean it in its
narrowest sense of book-learning in the classroom.
Her parents would not send her away to school even
now, though they once went so far as to look at a
school which they thought might be suitable. But her
sister was growing up apace and they could not bear
the idea of having no child running round the
house.

There is little doubt that the further education received in her home, through close companionship
with her parents, and their encouragement of her
best tastes and talents, helped to fit her for her future
life.

Again, the uninterrupted routine of outdoor games,
bicycling, riding, and driving, brought colour to her
cheeks and vigour to her limbs at a time when these
were most needed.

At Purley Hall, her next home near Pangbourne in
Berkshire, Olave began learning to swim and to row:
Ranger and Guide like activities which in those days
might so easily have been omitted from the ordinary
girl's school curriculum.

Peggy the pony had been sold and Olave was given
another, a little horse of her own, 'Tompy' by name,
for whose care and well-being she alone was res-

ponsible. No human being could have been served more faithfully than was Tompy by his adoring mistress, who sat up at night with him when he was ill and lavished on him a care and affection which few horses can have enjoyed.

'*Having given up all book-work,*' says Olave, '*I had more leisure for Tompy, for Doogy, my beloved spaniel, and the rest of my pets.*'

The Chief Guide owns that in those days she had not the slightest affection for books, and that this was a drawback when in later years she was called upon not only to read books but also to write them. Her dogged determination not to be beaten, and some literary ability inherited from her mother, however, have stood her in good stead.

Any sort of handcraft, housework, gardening, games, rowing and boat-handling, riding and driving, walking, and the care of animals, all these took pride of place.

One of the first duties of a Scout or Guide is to practise observation and deduction; or, to put it more plainly, to notice everything and try to find out its object or meaning. The Chief Guide is a most observant person and this may be due to the fact that she was (and is) keenly alive to things happening around her. On a train journey, for instance, when other people were reading to pass the time, she would be looking

eagerly out of the window, noticing anything or anybody a little out of the ordinary and trying to account
for them.

At Luscombe Castle, Dawlish, in Devonshire—a
house rented from Mr. Hoare, a London banker—
Olave had her first real seaside home. Here she could
have plenty of swimming practice, and on July 9th,
1904, recorded in her diary that she could *really swim
at last*.

This mastery of an element (such an important
item in Guiding), so that it no longer held any fears
for her, completed Olave's pleasure in her seaside
home, and many were the bathing and boating expeditions with young friends as well as with her own
family. Riding excursions on lovely Dartmoor with
other horse lovers were also great fun.

Another important happening in the year when
Olave was fifteen was her Confirmation by the
Bishop of Crediton at St. Michael's, Dawlish. This
event she took seriously, as she did most things, and
noted in her diary that it had been *a most important
day* for her. At her Confirmation she accepted
responsibility for her future life as a Christian and
citizen.

The Dawlish climate did not suit Mrs. Soames and
before the end of another year a house had been
found: Bradfield, near Cullompton. After a winter in

London, with a round of classes, lectures, picture galleries, and plays for the young people, the family moved to Bradfield in May 1905, when Olave was sixteen.

The motor-car was just making its first appearance, stirring the old sleepy existence of many a country place into a life of hustle and bustle. Enveloped in motoring caps and veils—for the cars were open and the roads dusty—the ladies of the family ventured into these strange, terrifying vehicles and were driven by the man of the family where no chauffeur was employed. In those days women had neither votes nor the 'right' to drive motor-cars!

Cars were not at first altogether popular among a horse-loving community.

*'A buzz, a whizz, a cloud of dust,*
*A loud blood-curdling yell;*
*A ghastly object flashing by,*
*Then silence—and a smell.'*

wrote 'Horse Lover' in a journal of the day.

But novelties soon develop into everyday affairs and it was not long before the Soames family bought a car and engaged a chauffeur to drive it. Motoring rather appealed to Olave, though her main delight continued to be in her horses and dogs. She confessed to her diary that she hated London and dreaded going there again, mainly because of having to leave Doogy behind.

Although she was enjoying life to the full, and knew herself to be a child of good fortune in having loving parents and a happy home life, Olave sometimes wondered—and confided the wonder to her diary—whether there was not more to life than having a good time. Was there something else that she ought to be doing?

'*Another year gone by and wasted*,' she commented, and yet at the moment there seemed no alternative to the life she was leading. Her parents would not willingly have allowed her to train for a career or to leave home. When she was seventeen, however, she did write privately to a hospital to find out about the possibility of training as a nurse. The reply came that she was too young. So she continued to be a good companion at home and especially to her father, for her older sister was now grown-up and, with their mother, often away in London.

How difficult it is today to guess whether a girl is fifteen or seventeen or twenty, or even more.

But in the days of which I am writing, before the First World War, it was not like that at all. People then grew up suddenly, overnight as it were. One day there would be a schoolgirl with pigtails or a horse's mane or a 'door-knocker' hanging down her back, and short skirts; and then, next day, the hair would have been put up, i.e. pinned round her head with hair-pins, the skirts let down to the ankles, and—behold—a young lady!

In Olave Soames's case the transition took place while she was living at Bradfield. On January 4th, 1907, her parents gave a dance at which she 'came out', and from that day onwards she took her place as a grown-up member of the family.

The year of growing up brought lots of fun and pleasure in the way of parties, tennis, picnics, and riding; but it had its dark days, too, for she lost her much-loved pet, Doogy, and was for a while almost inconsolable. She was sad, too, when the day came to leave Bradfield, a place which they had all grown to love and where Olave had made many good friends. But their lease had expired and Mr. Soames had taken another house near Bury St. Edmunds in Suffolk.

At Hardwick, in the cold winter of 1907, Olave added skating to her other accomplishments; she went at it 'all out', as with everything else that she enjoyed, and carried on skating at Prince's Club when next she had to stay for any time in London.

At Hardwick, too, she was able to ride regularly and to hunt; and she risked her neck several times a

week on a somewhat unruly horse which had been
lent to her. With her father she rode and drove and
played strenuous tennis and squash racquets, revelling
in this country life while her mother and sister were
enjoying the social round in London. Mrs. Soames
did not care for being what she called 'Suffolk-ated'
and always longed for the warmer south and to be
nearer London.

And now, at last, after years of wandering, Olave's
father had decided to buy a house and settle down.
One was found near Bournemouth, at Grey Rigg,
Lilliput, Parkstone, just inside Dorset.

It was in May 1908 that the family left Hardwick
for what Olave described as *our new home for
life*.

'. . . *it really is a delicious place, and has everything we
want—country, town, sea, sailing, people—and we are all
frightfully well here.*'

The house overlooked Poole Harbour where, a
few months earlier, on Brownsea Island, General
Baden-Powell had launched the Boy Scout scheme at
a trial camp.

During her four happy years at Grey Rigg, Olave
often sailed round the island, never dreaming of the

part that the Founder of Scouting was to play in her
future life or the part that she herself would be called
upon to play in his Movement.

In 1908 Scouting was in its infancy and the Girl
Guides unheard of, so she had not the urgent call to
service in that direction which came later to every
girl of leisure. She did undertake, with a friend, to
teach and amuse small boys once or twice a week in
a convalescent home run by the Invalid Children's
Aid Association. She stuck to this work nobly and
came to enjoy it and to have a real affection for the
children.

Apart from this effort at social service, Olave led at
Grey Rigg what she describes as a life of idle pleasure.
She certainly enjoyed it and, as was natural with a
charming and good-looking girl, had hosts of admir-
ers among the young men with whom she danced
and played games.

But she was in no particular hurry to marry,
resolving to wait until the right man came along, and
in the meantime to devote herself to her parents, who,
after her sister's marriage in 1911, were only too
thankful to have their cheerful young daughter with
them.

Olave was marking time, but she was not yet satisfied that she was fulfilling the real purpose of her life.
She had written in her diary:

' "*She by a river sat and sitting there*
  *She wept and made it deeper by a tear.*"

. . . is like me. *Fussing about and doing nothing all my life
is making about as much difference to the world at large as
Julia's tear to the depth of the river.*'

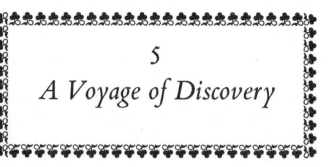

# 5
# A Voyage of Discovery

WHILE Olave Soames was—as she thought—idling away her life in Dorset, some strange events were taking place in the world outside.

General Baden-Powell, well known at that time as the heroic defender of Mafeking in the Boer War, had later been given the task of raising and commanding a police force known as the South African Constabulary.

In the Army he had trained his young soldiers in Scouting; when peace came he trained his mounted policemen to be good Scouts too; that is, to practise observation, deduction, tracking and pioneering, signalling by various methods, bridge-building, and all the other things so well known to Boy Scouts today. He had given them a uniform based on what he had worn on service, and it was both comfortable and practicable—a broad-brimmed hat, an open-necked shirt, and a green scarf.

When the General returned to England in 1903, to take up a new job as Inspector-General of Cavalry, he found to his surprise that the boys of Britain were not only forming themselves into patrols of Scouts but were also copying the uniform which he had worn in South Africa. They were using as a guide a little handbook which he had written for soldiers, called *Aids to Scouting*.

This would never do! He did not want to turn boys into soldiers and much of the book was unsuitable for them.

So, having proved at a trial camp on Brownsea Island that the Scouting scheme could be adapted for boys and that it really appealed to them, he rewrote the book, called it *Scouting for Boys*, and issued it in fortnightly parts, price fourpence each, so that even boys without much pocket-money could buy it.

In this he was helped by Mr. C. Arthur Pearson, a publisher and philanthropist.

The scheme caught on like wildfire and before the second instalment came out the countryside was dotted with patrols and troops of Boy Scouts, all looking to him as their Chief.

When he was invited to review the Boys' Brigade in Glasgow, General Baden-Powell suggested to Sir

William Smith, the Brigade's Founder, that he might find the Scouting programme of use as an extra activity for his boys; and many existing boys' movements, clubs, and churches did take up Scout training with great success.

There were, on the other hand, numbers of patrols and troops springing up quite outside any organization and these were finding their own Scoutmasters and demanding help and advice in their work.

There was nothing for it but to take a Headquarters Office, draw up some rules for them, and start a new Movement to be known as the Boy Scouts Association. The office secretary ordered a dozen Scout hats to sell to those boys who wrote asking where to get them; and that was the beginning of the Boy Scouts' Equipment Department with its branch shops in towns and cities today.

In 1909, nearly two years after the Brownsea Island camp, General Baden-Powell called a meeting of Scouts and a Conference of Scoutmasters, to be held at the Crystal Palace in South-East London. This immense glass building, which has since been destroyed by fire, had been set up in Hyde Park for the great Exhibition of 1851. Later the whole building was moved and re-erected at Sydenham as a permanent Exhibition site. Here were held all sorts of shows, band contests, meetings, and big firework

di．plays; it was a good centre for a big gathering of
Scouts.

General Baden-Powell went to the Crystal Palace
not knowing how many boys would turn up. To his
great surprise there were more than eleven thousand.

What surprised him still more was to find among
the Boy Scouts a party of girls dressed in Scout hats
and carrying staves, waiting hopefully to be inspected
with the boys.

Let one of these intrepid young women tell you in
her own words how she came to be there.

'*My older brother was a journalist*,' she writes, '*and
one day a paper-covered volume called* Scouting for Boys
*was given to him to review. . . . A friend and I decided that
by fair means or foul we would be Scouts. This proved
easier than we expected even if the means were not quite
fair. We simply registered at Scout Headquarters by using
initials instead of names, and my friend's mother agreed to
be our Scoutmistress, on condition she did not have to do
anything.*

'*For three months the Rabbit Patrol, Forest Mere Troop
(of two), lived Scouting. We built huts, followed tracks,
made bridges, chopped down trees, and cooked over smoky
camp-fires and thought we knew everything. We had
chosen the rabbit as our patrol emblem as they abounded in
the district and were easy to observe, but, unless in pain, a*

rabbit makes no noise, so we had to become foxes instead and went about barking at each other like demented dogs.

'In the spring of 1909 we felt that other girls should have the chance of playing this new game and, as our house lay mid-way between the two villages, we set out to interview the principals of the local schools and both willingly agreed to announce that any girls of the right age, interested in Scouting, would be welcome at our house on Saturday afternoon. I shall never forget that Saturday. Would anyone turn up, or would the two-and-a-half mile tramp be too great a deterrent? Would the "dampers" we planned to make be eatable? Would the weather keep fine?

'And then across the moorland tracks we spied a little group of girls coming from each direction, four from each village, the nucleus of two patrols. Although our numbers grew to nearly twenty we always kept to two patrols.

'The first day was definitely a success and during the following months the troop gained in strength and efficiency. As I held the St. John Ambulance certificate I taught all the first-aid and I must have had the reputation of never being satisfied. I remember questioning my corporal about her splinting of a fractured leg with a branch cut from a tree: "Suppose there were no trees handy, what else could you use?" Maggie went through the list, an umbrella, rolled newspaper, a poker, ending with "Anyway, accidents must happen convenient-like sometimes."

'Towards the end of the summer, a notice was published

in the Scout periodical to the effect that the Chief would review Scouts at the Crystal Palace in September. Needless to say my friend and I were wild to go but our Scoutmistress refused point blank to take any active part. However she agreed to take us to town for the night and to send us to the Palace by car. There was no official uniform but our troop wore Scout shirts and home-made khaki skirts and green scarves, the ends of which flapped in the breeze as a sign that we had performed a good turn!

'It was a cold wet day and our first contact with Scouting was not encouraging for, instead of a welcome, we were told firmly by one of the Marshals to "Go home, you can't come into the arena." We hung about for a bit and then a troop of boys marched in, followed by a small party of girls, and without hesitation we attached ourselves to this little band —and we were IN. No one took any notice of the two interlopers and to this day I have no idea which troop unknowingly adopted us, but we knew our drill and I am sure we were no disgrace.'

'Who are you?' asked the Chief Scout.

And the reply was: 'We are the Girl Scouts.'

Now the Chief was in a quandary. He did not want to damp the enthusiasm and spoil the fun of those girls who were so determined to do what their brothers were doing; and he knew that there was much in the Scout Law and Promise, and in the ideals of the

'A Guide is a friend to all and a sister to every other Guide'

A Guide P.T. display in India

*The Chief Guide inspects Wolf Cubs at a Mission in Western Australia*

*Guide headquarters in many parts of the world take their names from Pax Hill. The Chief Guide arrives to open 'Paxwold' in Western Australia*

Movement, which could be just as useful to girls as to boys. He was a little anxious, though, about what the parents might say, and also to have girls going about dressed as Scouts might make Scouting look childish, and this would harm the boys' Movement.

So he turned to one of his best friends—his sister— and asked her to help him to devise a 'sister Movement' for the girls, which would neither shock their parents nor make the boys feel that Scouting was a 'kid's game'.

Miss Agnes Baden-Powell was very ready to help; she had grown up in the reign of Queen Victoria and she felt quite sure that parents would not want their daughters turned into tomboys. She thought that what girls chiefly needed was training in housework, cooking, and nursing, and such things as would enable them to make comfortable homes for their husbands and children.

With the help of her brother she wrote two little booklets and called them 'Pamphlet A' and 'Pamphlet B'.

Pamphlet A was so arranged that it could be folded into a sort of letter-card and posted with a halfpenny stamp. It stated that eight thousand girls had already taken up Scouting and were carrying out boys' games and practices. A list of badges to be won in subjects more suitable for girls was appended and it was said

C

that any girl obtaining eighteen of these would be awarded a 'Silver Fish'.

Pamphlet B gave further details of instruction and also reproduced a scandalized letter from a parent to a daughter who had taken up Scouting.

Patrol names were to be in future, not Wolves, Bears, or Otters, like the boys', but such titles as Cornflowers, Roses, or Fuchsias. And—most important of all—the name of the new Movement was to be not Scouts but Guides.

The Chief Scout explained to the girls that, instead of merely copying men, women should lead them, or be their guides. Guides were people who knew the way and could show it to others.

As you can imagine, this change of name and programme was not at first very popular with girls who had been Scouts. They had revelled in their Scouting and were rather lukewarm about being Guides. The Owls and Foxes kept their original patrol cries because, as they explained, Sunflowers and Pimpernels did not make any nice noises.

At first it seemed that the girls' early enthusiasm might die down under the new regime, and the whole Movement fizzle out.

That was how matters stood when, in January 1912, General Sir Robert Baden-Powell (he had been knighted in 1910) started out on a World Tour to see the Boy Scouts overseas, who, he had heard, were taking up Scouting every bit as keenly as those at home.

His ship, the *Arcadian*, left Southampton on January 3rd, and in it went two other people who were destined to play a big part in the Girl Guide Movement.

One of these was Mrs. Juliette Low. She was an American woman who had married an Englishman and who spent her time partly in Great Britain and partly in the United States. While in England she had met General Baden-Powell and had become very enthusiastic about the Girl Guide scheme. She had actually run a Company of Guides in London and started another near her Scottish home; and she was now on her way to start the Movement going in the United States. That was the beginning of the Girl Scouts of America, who, though they never changed their name to Girl Guides, are all part and parcel of the girls' World Association, and a very big and important part today.

The other person was Olave Soames, who, with her father, was bound for Jamaica and sunshine.

'*There is only one interesting person in this ship*', she wrote home, '*and that is General Baden-Powell, the Scout man.*'

It had been a cold grey morning when Olave and her father arrived at Southampton, and there was a dock strike. The passengers for the pleasure cruise were to be taken out by tender to the *Arcadian*, whose maiden voyage this was, lying out in deep water.

There was quite a long wait for the boat train with last-minute passengers to arrive, and while the early comers hung about in the chilly mist a troop of Boy Scouts—not then so common a sight in public places as today—appeared. These smartly turned-out youngsters had come to say '*Bon voyage*' to their Chief as he set out on this first World Tour; they were lined up and duly inspected by him—one boy receiving a Life Saving Medal at his hands—which naturally attracted quite a lot of attention.

This little scene made a great impression on Olave and she hoped that she might have a chance of getting to know this unusual man who, though a world-renowned soldier, could yet take such a warm, personal interest in ordinary boys.

When a mutual friend introduced them, the Chief Scout said to Olave: 'This is not the first time I have seen you.'

Olave was puzzled. She had followed his brilliant career and had worn his portrait as a buttonhole badge at the time of the Siege of Mafeking, but she could not remember any previous meeting.

They put two and two together at last and found that they had both been in London in 1910 and living quite close to each other in Kensington. At that time the Chief had been writing some articles in *The Scout* on how people's characters could often be partly determined by their manner of walking; and, as he walked through Kensington Gardens on his way to Knightsbridge Barracks, he had noted—with his habitual keen observation—the slim, upright figure with its firm and purposeful tread.

'But didn't you have a dog with you—a spaniel?' he asked.

It was true. On that visit to London in 1910 Olave had been able to take Doogy the Second with her, and that had made all the difference to her appreciation of London.

That was the first coincidence of many. As they sat talking together, while the Chief Scout sketched, they discovered that they had both been born on February 22nd, and that they shared many ideals.

It was a happy voyage, and by the time the *Arcadian* reached Jamaica they were engaged.

Then the Chief sailed away to fulfil his Scouting programme and Olave returned home with her father to spend her last summer at Grey Rigg.

She had some months to wait before the Chief's return from his long tour, but they were happy

months because she could see a new world opening
out to her. She knew all about the Scouts and Guides,
and her future husband's hopes of what the Movement might do for the boys and girls of the Empire
now that he had retired from the Army in order to
take charge of the Movement.

Olave had listened, feeling that here at last was the
chance she had been looking for of doing something
really worth while. And this opportunity was being
handed to her by the one man in the world that she
felt she would like to marry!

Meantime he was travelling farther and farther away
from her and they had to be content with letters.
Olave also followed the Chief's moves through
the daily Press and learned of his visits to Scouts
in Canada and the States, Australia, New Zealand,
and other countries on the way.

So the months went by until in the late summer he
came home. On October 30th, 1912, there was a
quiet wedding at St. Peter's Church, Parkstone, and
Olave left the seventeenth home of her girlhood to
make a new home for her husband.

The marriage of their Chief came as a blow to
some of his Scouts, who felt that now he would not
have so much time to devote to them and their
affairs. They bombarded him with indignant letters.

The Chief reassured them. Not only would he be

as keen as ever on Scouting but he would also be able to give more time to it. His wife would help him, and so would the fine new motor-car—presented by the Scouts.

The Scouts forgave him and conferred on Lady Baden-Powell the title of 'The Lady Chief'.

What the Girl Guides thought about it all is not recorded, but probably they felt that some good might even come their way as a result of their Chief's marriage.

It did—but that good was still to come.

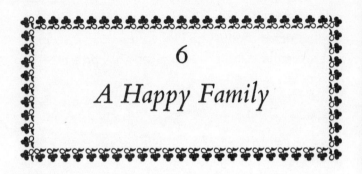

# 6

# *A Happy Family*

FOR months the Chief Scout had been overworking and his doctor had warned him that he must take a real rest and holiday. To do this at home, where Scouts were everywhere depending on him, would have been impossible. He decided to take his wife for a few weeks to Algeria—right into the desert, and far away from Scouts and Guides and letters and telephones.

Off they went, in the middle of January 1913, on a delayed honeymoon. The Chief could not resist visiting the Gibraltar Scouts, but very soon after this visit civilization was far behind them. They pitched their camp out in the desert, cooked their own food, slept under the stars, went for long tramps, and revelled in every minute of it.

Here in the desert Olave was put through her paces

and the Chief discovered that she had the makings of a good Scout and a first-rate camper.

The Boy Scouts at her old home—Parkstone—had asked if they might take the title of 'Lady Baden-Powell's Own', and when the B-Ps got back to England—having gone ashore at Malta to see the Scouts there—they went to Grey Rigg and inspected these Parkstone boys.

Talking to them the Chief Scout said of his wife:

*'You see a lady in a beautiful black hat and white coat. I saw her not so long ago scrubbing out a saucepan. We were living the simple life in the desert. We had only one pan and that was a saucepan, and it had to be used for frying our fish and also for boiling our coffee. After the lady had done the fish she had to get grass roots and sand and scrub the pot out so that we could make our coffee in it. The lady did it well—and she also did the washing. But I think I must stand up for the Scouts and for the mere man and tell you that she had to fall back on me to do the ironing.'*

Anybody who knows the Chief Guide will have not the slightest doubt that her saucepan was always shining, both inside and outside, although she could not go to a shop to buy a patent cleanser. There were no shops in the desert, but there was plenty of sand, and plenty of grit in its user!

One of the most important things in Scouting and Guiding is to be able to make bricks without straw, or, as that wise man Rudyard Kipling put it, to be able to do

> *'The work that lies under your nose*
> *With the tools that lie under your hand.'*

In those days camping by women and girls was quite unusual, though Guides, of course, were beginning to do it. Some girls I know borrowed their brother's tents on his return from a Boundary Commission in West Africa. They pitched them on Norland Moor in the West Riding of Yorkshire, and were thought by their friends and relations to be doing something not only ridiculous but positively dangerous.

Those Girl Scouts and Girl Guides of early days were certainly pioneers. To modern Rangers and Guides their photographs, showing them in large hats and carrying poles, seem very laughable. But we ought to feel deeply grateful to them, for they were opening up to girls everywhere a life of greater freedom and happiness in the open air. But it all took time.

Even six years later, in an address to a Girl Guide meeting, the Founder was compelled to say:

'*There is an increasing need for training our girls for something more than hem-stitching or piano-playing.*'

For a married lady, the wife of a General, to choose to scrub saucepans in camp when she could have stayed in a luxury hotel, was an unheard-of thing.

\*            \*            \*

But now the holiday was over and the Baden-Powells were busy settling into their new home, Ewhurst Place, in East Sussex. Here in due course the three children were born.

Ewhurst Place was the big house in a tiny village. Standing on a hill, it overlooked Bodiam Castle and a magnificent stretch of Sussex and Kent countryside. To reach it from London you took a train to Roberts-bridge and changed there on to a tiny branch railway 'The Kent and East Sussex', which ran from Roberts-bridge to Headcorn, alighting at Bodiam, an inter-mediate station. From the station, if no car was handy, a short cut led through fields to the house. In front of the house were wide terraced lawns where on warm summer nights the Chiefs and their visitors could sleep out on camp-beds—without even a tent.

We cannot picture the Chief Guide idling away her time, even in the depths of the country; and she was certainly not idle at Ewhurst, though her occupations and interests differed as much from those of her earlier life as they did from those of today. Now she had no time for tennis and very little for violin-playing; instead, she created a fine home for the Chief to return to after his many long and exacting journeys in the cause of Scouting. Frequently she accompanied him on these tours and was always in demand for pinning on badges or presenting prizes at Scout shows.

In between times she learned to drive the car and to type; when proficient she typed the Chief's articles and books and drove him round the countryside. She spent many spare minutes in polishing the car, for it would never do for the Chief to arrive at a Scout Rally in a mud-stained vehicle.

And then there was always the garden and gardening!

People who live in towns sometimes imagine that there is not much to do in the country; nothing could be further from the truth. At Ewhurst there was always something going on, and whatever was going on the Chief's wife was in the thick of it, whether it was a village concert or arranging the church flowers, or housing and transporting visiting clergy and Scouts, or getting on friendly terms with the local inhabitants and giving tea parties for them.

Olave started up a Scout troop in Ewhurst village and ran it in partnership with their chauffeur until he left to join the Royal Flying Corps (now the R.A.F.). From her experiences gained in this way she spoke at a number of meetings of lady Scoutmasters and, as the Chief's wife, received a right royal welcome from them and from Scouts everywhere.

Writing in the *Boy Scouts Headquarters Gazette* (now *The Scouter*) in 1913, Lady Baden-Powell suggested that it was unnecessary for lady Scout-masters to wear uniform, and recommended instead a short tweed skirt and Norfolk jacket. '*For*', she said, '*the usual ladies' dress is not sufficiently practical, while uniform tends towards our looking like Girl Guide captains.*'

From which it will be seen that in 1913 her Lady-ship was still at heart a Boy Scout rather than a Girl Guide!

This was not really very surprising, for the Scouts had taken her to their own hearts and she shone in the reflected glory of B-P. When the boys could not have their beloved Chief they were quite ready to welcome the person nearest to him, the one who bore his name and shared his deep interest in their welfare.

That feeling still exists today. Now that their Founder is no longer with them, the Scouts of the Commonwealth regard the present Chief Scout as their beloved leader and example in Scouting; but on Lady Baden-Powell the Scouts of the world will always lean as the closest living link with their great Founder; and her appearance on the platform at any Scout gathering is the signal for an immense burst of clapping and spontaneous cheering. Like their sisters the Guides, they love and revere her not only for what she is and does but for the name she bears so nobly.

On the anniversary of his parents' wedding day Peter was born, and seldom, I suppose, has any son of non-royal parents received such a welcome into the world. Hundreds of telegrams had been received before he was many hours old, and for days and weeks congratulations flowed in.

The baby was baptized Arthur Robert Peter, the first name after his godfather, the Duke of Connaught, the second for his father, and the third for himself. The christening took place at St. Peter's, Parkstone, where his parents had been married.

He grew into an attractive small person with flaming hair and a most beguiling smile which was always forthcoming in spite of the childish illnesses and setbacks which at first caused his parents some anxiety.

When Peter was nearly two his sister Heather appeared on the scene—and was soon another fascinating red poll. Heather's christening party at Ewhurst was a very grand affair, with Scouts and Guides lining the route to and from the church and the whole village invited to tea on the lawn. The Guides who helped to form the Guard of Honour were from Roedean School and they wore Scout hats and carried staves!

Heather took her second name of Grace from her grandmother, Henrietta Grace Baden-Powell. Peter had been a great joy to old Mrs. B-P, but she did not live to see her grand-daughter and namesake.

So now the Chiefs had a boy and a girl of their own on whom later they would be able to practise the Scout and Guide ideas which they were now promoting.

But in 1915 the First World War was raging in France and everyone at home was anxious to do his or her bit in helping to win it.

There could be no peace at Ewhurst while the boom of the guns across the Channel could be so regularly heard.

The Scouts had raised money for a Recreation Hut for the troops in France, and the Mercers' Company had given another—and both were to be staffed by Scout workers. Obviously these would have to be ladies or older men, as all the young fit men were otherwise engaged. The Chief had been to France to see his regiment, the 13th Hussars, and now Lady Baden-Powell decided to go over and lend a hand in the Hut work.

Uniform for lady Scoutmasters and Cubmasters was still under consideration at home, but for service overseas it was essential to wear it, as the Scout uniform had been accorded official recognition by the authorities. So, wearing a Scout hat, khaki suit and shirt, and green tie, Lady Baden-Powell left for France in October, having seen the two babies and their nurse safely established with her mother at Grey Rigg.

Here, in her own words, is a sketch of her life as a 'bar maid'—somewhere in France.

*'It is hardly light yet, and a raw cold creeps through the little draughty house. Mimi the kitten is mewing to be let out of her night quarters and Jock the Airedale is sniffing at the door, eager to go and keep guard over Boots the rabbit.*

*'We had four boxes of matches about the place overnight, but in the early dawn it is difficult to find even one. I get the box and handle out the cinders from the grate in the kitchen range, scrape out the ashes and lay the new fire. With a chopper as blunt as a brick one splits the fire-sticks. A touch of paraffin, a layer of cinders to prevent the fire being swamped by the wet black grit which passes for coal,*

*a flaring newspaper in the flue to start an updraught, and the fire is under way. Pots and kettles are put on the hot plate for early tea and bathwater, and one has breathing space in which to sweep out the kitchen, fold the towels and clothes which have been hanging to dry overnight, and to get to work with the scraping knife and brushes on the shoes which, too, have been recovering in the oven from last night's tramp through the eternal mud of the camp.*

'I am orderly today. The three of us take it in turn to get up early and do the housework and cooking in our little cottage near the camp.

'At ten comes our first turn of duty at the bar. Men, tired already from several hours' work, come hurrying in for a steaming cup of cocoa or tea during the half hour's law that is allowed. We hand out brimming cups continuously, and then quite suddenly the hut is empty again and we have time to clean up and get ready for the next lot. . . .

'The building consists of a big hall with a very good stage at one end and the bar at the other. Behind the stage is the silence room and library, while behind the bar are the offices, mess-room and sleeping rooms for the men of the staff, and kitchen, store-room, etc. Along the outside is a verandah where in summer the men can sit and watch their fellow-workers playing games in the field beyond; while inside the hut are chairs and tables for the men to write letters on. Sunday is the great letter-writing day and the room is full all the afternoon, and silence reigns supreme

*as they send their messages to those they have left behind
them.*

*          *          *

'*At half past twelve we have another rush. They have
had their dinners but they come to us for that little extra—
a mug of cocoa or tea and very often two big hunks of cake.
The pouring out becomes a sort of race. Will the tea in the
urn last out; and will the supply of cups run out before the
formidable queue of patient waiting men has come to an
end? Each one has a smile and a little nod of good morning
for me—they are so cheery and nice.*

'"*Good morning, Miss, another of those cakes same as
you gave me yesterday, please,*"—*as if one could remember
among the hundreds of others. As it happened I luckily remembered this man and his taste because he had such a
cheery smile and I thought him like a Boy Scout. I asked
him later, when I got to know him, whether he had been.
No, he had only been in the Fire Brigade. But I think he
will be in the Scouts one day!*

'"*Good morning, milady. I was Patrol Leader in the
——— Troop of Scouts. Last time I saw you was at Bir-
mingham.*" *I remembered him too for he had been in
Hospital there and we had been to see him. And this was
one of many. It is so nice when ex-Scouts come to have a
chat; and many also come to tell me of the doings of their
little sons who are in the Scouts.*

'A very much thumbed notebook is produced from a grimy tunic, and a rather faded photo is handed across the counter for me to see. "That's my little Johnny at home, he's in your Corps," says a gruff voice, and a man nods towards my Scout hat. "And he tells me he's just got his second-class badge."

' "Please, ma'am, can I have a private talk with you?" I explain that I am here for such purposes. "Yes, how can I help?"

' "Well, it's this way. I haven't heard good news from home. My wife writes that the rent has been raised. She has got the kiddies to look after too. Who ought the Missus to see about it?" And so on.

'But the hardest work comes in the evenings, especially if it be, as it generally is now, a wet and freezing night. The men come out of their thin windy tents in the dark, through the slosh and sleet to get warmth and light and dry standing room, if only for an hour or two. They have worked all day and now they flock into this great room to smoke and chat with friends. Their clothes are as dirty as you like from the workshops and the mud.

'The atmosphere becomes somewhat stifling; but it is great to see the happy crowd of men enjoying their evening under this roof. They are so well-behaved and jolly; and so grateful for the little we can do to make their life here more bearable.

'Sometimes there is a concert and the hall is packed from

end to end with a critical but wildly enthusiastic audience. On other days there is just a ceaseless hum of talk. The day's news is read out by the Hut Leader and this is listened to eagerly and attentively while you could hear a pin drop, though before and after it the place is a veritable babel.

'As bed-time draws near our busy time begins. There is a steady move towards the urns of hot drinks, and we have to "hustle some" until the dreadful moment when the lights are put out and reluctant buyers are sent away by reluctant sellers.

'And then we splosh back to our little cottage, made happy by the thought of the friendly little chats one has had —little words of no great meaning perhaps but with a world of good-fellowship in them. The fact that one is here solely to try and help them in "doing their bit" is I think appreciated. One said to me not long ago: "You don't know what it has meant to us chaps to have you ladies here."

'Then I felt it had been worth while to leave home and babies to try to do my little bit.'

So the winter in France wore on. The three months for which she had originally gone stretched to four. Replacements were slow in coming. Another Scout Hut had been opened and required staff. Lady Baden-Powell was tired out and had suffered a bad attack of the prevailing 'flu before the reinforcements arrived. At last the day came to return to England, home, and babies, and she left France satisfied that the Huts were well established with supplies of workers coming along.

Ewhurst in the spring seemed wonderful, and the babies had grown out of all recognition. The primroses were flowering in Sussex. Only the guns still booming across the water prevented home from being a place of complete peace and joy.

Before the war ended another little daughter, Betty St. Clair, rounded off the Chief's family. Betty was born on April 16th, 1917, and was quite unlike the other two; her hair was very dark like her mother's. Though small, she was beautifully proportioned, like a little black-haired doll, and with a clear, pale skin.

But before Betty's arrival two momentous decisions had been made. They would leave Ewhurst for a warmer climate, and Lady Baden-Powell was enrolled as a Girl Guide.

# 7
# *Guiding*

THE Girl Guide Movement had been in existence for six years before Lady Baden-Powell came into it. There were several reasons for this.

Up to the time of her marriage in 1912 she had barely heard of the Girl Guides. From then onwards, however, she had learned all about this, her husband's 'second child'. If she were going to lift any part of the double load from his burdened shoulders the girls—not the boys—ought to be her responsibility.

One obvious reason why she hung back was that she had to give her time and energy to her home and her own small children. Home duties must come first.

Secondly, her mother, of whom she was extremely fond, had a rooted objection to uniform for girls or women. She was herself a beautiful woman who draped, rather than dressed, herself in flowing gowns and immense picture hats. The very name of Girl Guide was anathema to her and she never came to appreciate or realize the value of Guide training.

For years after she became Chief Guide Lady Baden-Powell used to remove her uniform before going to see her mother, and could never mention in her presence the subject uppermost in her mind. This was a very real grief to Olave, for the two had always been very close in affection and sympathy.

Another difficulty lay in the fact that Miss Agnes Baden-Powell—the Founder's sister—had very naturally and rightly selected the members of the Girl Guide Committee mainly from among her own friends. These belonged to an older generation inclined to view with suspicion too exuberant youth.

Parents were haunted by the fear that their daughters might be turned into what they called 'tomboys' instead of young ladies, and the Committee were determined to safeguard the Movement from any such accusation. A debt of gratitude is due to these women, for if Guiding had come suddenly instead of gradually to their notice the parents might have vetoed it altogether.

In September 1914, however, Lady Baden-Powell had approached the Headquarters office with an offer of help. The result, which she recorded in her diary, was that *the Committee prefers to do its work without me*.

Having made the gesture, she now felt that, as there was obviously no place at Headquarters for an untried and inexperienced worker, she could with a clear conscience return to her first love—the Boy Scouts.

But the Chief Scout was by no means satisfied to let the matter rest there. His wife was helping him enormously behind the scenes, as an extra typist and chauffeuse, but he knew that she had it in her to do a far bigger job than that. He also knew, however, that, once involved, she would plunge in up to the neck. Olave never did anything by halves, and he was not inclined to press her too hard all at once.

It was in the spring of 1916, on her return from her service in France, that Lady Baden-Powell decided to begin at the other end. Instead of trying to assist at Headquarters, she would work up the Guides in her own county of Sussex. This would prove her fitness or otherwise for leadership, and Headquarters agreed to issue her with a warrant as Commissioner for Sussex.

Reorganization of the whole Guide Movement was in the air. The splendid war work done by the Guides had put them on a better footing with the public; the Founder decided that the time had come to obtain for the Movement a Charter of Incorporation.

In Sussex there were already a few scattered Companies of Guides and these were only too thankful to have the help of their Founder's wife. There were no Commissioners and no organization to support the captains, who were nevertheless carrying on with enthusiasm their work of training the Guides.

It was an uphill job that Lady Baden-Powell had let herself in for; in 1916 most people were completely immersed in war work of one sort or another. Naturally it was difficult to persuade them to look beyond the present and consider the future of the children being brought up under the shadow of war.

Olave determined to make Sussex a model of Guide organization which other counties—equally unorganized—could copy. To do this she travelled the length and breadth of the county by car, bicycle, train, or bus. She called on people likely to help, inspected the little scattered Companies of keen girls, encouraging them to form themselves into local associations and come together for joint meetings.

Armed with a parliamentary map of the county, she pored over this, writing to people of any standing in each particular neighbourhood, begging them to become Commissioners or secretaries. There were an enormous number of refusals, for not only were women absorbed in the more immediate work but, even if they had heard of it, they thought very little of the Girl Guide Movement. There were, however,

just a few acceptances and these encouraged Lady
Baden-Powell to keep on trying.

At that time she typed literally hundreds of letters
explaining what it was all about and urging and re-
urging people to give it their support. When they
refused by letter, but left any possible loophole, she
went to see them and often won them to her side by
her charm and enthusiasm.

It was gruelling work involving cross-country
journeys. A typical day in May 1916 is thus recorded
in her diary:

'*See Heathfield Guide workers, also Lewes. Lunch at
Burgess Hill and inspect Guides and Scouts there and at
Hurstpierpoint. Tea there. Visit Guide in hospital at
Brighton. Stay night at Roedean School and talk to girls on
Guide work.*'

Day after day, week after week, and month after
month, her diary showed entries like that.

In October of the same year a Conference of Commissioners was held at Matlock, which both the Chief
and Lady Baden-Powell attended. The latter wore a
home-made uniform consisting of a navy-blue coat
(with silk facings) and skirt, a Guide's hat turned up
at the left side, and a Guide belt. Some of the Com-

missioners present had also got themselves into uniform of a sort; others came in ordinary dress.

This Conference was certainly a turning point for the Guide Movement and, as such, takes its place in history. By the unanimous vote of all the Commissioners present Lady Baden-Powell was appointed Chief Commissioner of Guides for the British Empire. Eighteen months later she was appointed Chief Guide.

Now indeed she had plunged in up to the neck.

Today, when the Chief Guide goes to a Rally or meeting, all that she has to do is to appear in the right place at the right moment, to take the salute and talk to the assembled Guides.

In 1916 it was very different. Not only had she to appear at the Rally in the guise of Inspecting Officer but from the other end she had to organize the affair, tell the Commissioners what was expected of them, and, indeed, bring the whole thing into being.

She had indeed many good helpers and allies, some of whom had been longer in the Movement and could advise her. It would be invidious to single out names, but friends and helpers were added almost daily, though the main responsibility was hers. As, one by one, the counties fell into line with their quota of County, Division, and District Commissioners, she marked them in on a great map. Now, instead of

perambulating Sussex, she had to travel to every part
of the United Kingdom, organizing, urging, and encouraging people to take up work for the Guides.
Even if she could not fill in all the gaps immediately
she determined to have the framework complete so
that when people were released from their war jobs
they would find a place awaiting them.

That was in fact what happened. When at last the
war ended in 1918 numbers of leaders of the right
type came in ready to give of their best to the Guides
as they had given it to the Women's Services in the
war. Such women as Dame Katharine Furse and Dame
Helen Gwynne-Vaughan, and many who, like them,
had held high rank in the Services, were proud now
to serve under the Chief Guide. That this should be so
was an immense tribute to her personality and gift of
leadership.

In 1917 the first list of Commissioners was published by Guide Headquarters. The number had risen
from almost nothing to 166. During Lady Baden-
Powell's term of office as Chief Commissioner it rose
to nearly three thousand.

The move to Little Mynthurst Farm happened
when Betty was a month or two old, and once more
Olave was hard at work making a comfortable home
for the family as well as carrying out her duties as
Chief Commissioner and Chief Guide.

It was only a temporary lease and during their eighteen months there the B-Ps were on the look-out for a permanent home. Ewhurst had been rather too cold and damp in winter and farther from London than suited the comings and goings which were now required of them both.

Little Mynthurst, though a quaint house with a happy old-world atmosphere, had certain distinct drawbacks. It was full of low beams which constantly came in contact with the Chief's head; the old floors had cracks and holes in them; and in winter the pipes burst and the chimneys smoked; and the surrounding country was not so attractive as that they had left behind at Ewhurst. But while the babies were small it was an ideal setting and near enough to London to make meetings and office work comparatively accessible. Petrol was rationed and many journeys in those days had to be done by bicycle or train instead of by car.

I think the Chief Guide's favourite literature at that period of her life was *Bradshaw's Railway Guide*—a tome scarcely remembered today and an art in itself to master. Many and complicated were the cross-country journeys which she performed in pursuit of Guide workers.

While at Little Mynthurst the Chief Scout finished the writing of a new handbook, called *Girl Guiding*, to replace his sister's earlier one; and Lady Baden-Powell wrote a companion volume called *Training Girls as Guides*.

From Ewhurst in 1916 she had published a booklet called *The Girl Guide Movement*, giving information about organization and the duties of Commissioners, based on her Sussex experience. But this was her first real book. She who had never attempted authorship, and whose early writings had been limited to diaries and letters, now found that in the interests of the Movement she must write books. Truly, a Guide must be able to turn her hand to anything!

The Chief Guide has always preferred speaking to writing, and listening to reading. She still finds the churning out of books, articles, and 'messages' a far greater effort than merely addressing a few thousand people personally or by radio; but few would guess this, for, like everything else she does, she gives her whole mind to it and puts all of herself into her writing just as she does into her speaking. But it is the personal touch that she believes in and continually urges upon others. '*Go and see her—a personal interview is worth any number of letters*' is one of her watchwords. And in this she is certainly an example.

During their time at Little Mynthurst the Chief Guide accomplished a mission rather outside her normal work. She was selected to go to France to investigate conditions in the Women's Auxiliary Army Corps, and there spent a busy week. Besides carrying out her investigation and reporting on it, she revisited her old haunts and relived her days in the Army Huts, which she found were still going strong and had been enlarged and improved. The Guides had raised enough money to provide another Recreation Hut and also a motor-ambulance for the Army in France.

In 1918 the Chief Guide began to tackle the organization of Guiding overseas. She formed an Imperial Council in London, as well as an International Council. Cut off from the parent Movement by war, these branches were growing and spreading rapidly and were feeling the need of a link-up under some central body. The International Council, starting as a body of friendly correspondents from London to the various countries, became the nucleus of the present-day World Association of Girl Guides and Girl Scouts.

On November 11th, 1918, came the longed-for Armistice and the world was at peace. London went mad, as it had not done since Mafeking Night, and while colonial troops were holding high revel in Trafalgar Square the B-Ps spent the day quietly at home, rejoicing in the end of the so-called 'war to end all wars'.

Two days later, on November 13th, they started
out on a house-hunting expedition in a corner of
England which had its appeal for them both.

Bicycling to Betchworth station, they took their
machines by train to Farnham. They rode round
looking at various houses recommended by the house
agent. None of these seemed suitable and then almost
by chance, and on the last-minute recommendation
of some distant relations, they went on to Bentley
and looked at a house called 'Blackacre' at the top of
a long drive.

The site was ideal and the house, facing south, was
well away from the main road. They decided on the
spot—eating their picnic lunch on the drive—that
they would buy it and change its name from
Blackacre to Pax Hill, in honour of the Armistice
and of the Scout and Guide ideal of peace through
friendship.

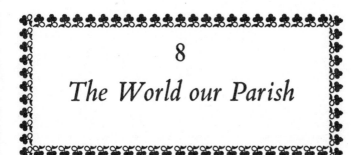

# 8

# *The World our Parish*

WORK, laughter, and sunshine; the rhythmic cawing of rooks and the cooing of pigeons; the scent of sweetbriar, lavender, and pinks; the taste of honey; and the nimble footsteps of growing children.

Pax Hill! The very name spells magic to so many people in so many lands, for in the twenty years that the Baden-Powells lived in it their visitors must have numbered thousands, and certainly more letters from distant lands found their way to this house than to all the other houses in the village put together.

To their ordinary neighbours in that part of Hampshire—Pax Hill stands in Hampshire though on the Surrey border—it was just a pleasant, modern red-brick house, and a house from which its owners were often regrettably absent for months on end; but to the Scout and Guide world Pax Hill—like Baden-Powell—was a name to conjure with.

Today there are many Baden-Powell houses in different parts of the world, as well as the large central one in London. There are also Baden-Powell streets and avenues and drives—and even a Baden-Powell mountain. There are also Pax Hills, Pax Houses, Pax Tors, Pax Wolds, and Pax almost anything you can think of, which have taken their names from that one house.

Unlike the Chief Guide's present home at Hampton Court Palace, Pax Hill has made the whole of its history in the short space of fifty years.

Built by Mr. Trimmer, a partner in Payne's Toy Shop in Holborn, London, in 1908, it was sold by his widow ten years later to the Baden-Powells. Having changed its original name of Blackacre to Pax Hill, they moved in with the three children early in 1919. The house then became not merely a home for their personal family but also a gathering place for Scout and Guide folk from near by or far afield. It was the centre from which the spirit of Scouting and Guiding seemed to radiate, and it was the ambition of every member to go there if only for a few hours in order to catch something of that spirit.

Owing to the late war, when nations had been cut off from one another, it had not been generally realized how deeply the Scout and Guide Movements had taken root and to what proportions it had grown in other countries.

The first World Jamboree of Scouts, held at Olympia, London, in 1920, brought a large-scale invasion of Scouts to Britain and many of these made tracks for Pax Hill to see how and where their great Chief lived. He had just been acclaimed by them CHIEF SCOUT OF ALL THE WORLD.

This Jamboree was followed by another, at Wembley in 1924, and the same year saw the first World Camp of Girl Guides at Foxlease in the New Forest.

Pax Hill was right on the route, whether for people arriving by ship at Southampton and travelling to London, or for those going to London from the New Forest. The resources of the Chiefs' ever hospitable house were often strained to the utmost in giving a welcome to the leaders and members of the two branches of the Movement.

The lawn, large enough for two tennis courts, was more often occupied by tents; the summer-house and the caravan, as well as every bedroom, had at times their quota of guests; and on both sides of the half-mile drive were to be seen, beneath shading trees, the little bivouacs of overnight camping visitors.

All were welcome, and many were the mugs of

cocoa handed out at the side door to campers whose uniform covered a multitude of differing nationalities, occupations, and religions, but who were all bound by the same Promise and Law.

Scarcely a day passed without visitors when the B-Ps were in residence; sometimes people with well-known names; sometimes a small Scout or Guide recuperating after an illness or accident; sometimes leaders of the Movement from overseas; often people whom it was hoped to enmesh in the great game. All were treated as part of the family and encouraged to take their share in whatever outdoor activity was in progress. It might be hedge-cutting, or painting, or bonfiring, or taking a swarm of bees, or a hundred and one other occupations which took them into the open air. One and all went away thrilled with their experience of staying with the Chiefs.

Yet, beyond and behind all this, each visitor had a feeling of being under observation, and a suspicion that, whether he or she liked it or not, each one was being gathered up and swept into the meshes of the Chiefs' purpose to play some part, however small, in its fulfilment.

In the midst of all this concourse of people the three young Baden-Powells spent a calm and happy childhood, in blissful ignorance of what did not immediately concern them. They lived in a world of their own, a world of wooden horses and live ponies, cats and dogs—and Caesar the donkey, first favourite.

They had their sunny nurseries and their sand-house in which to play, as well as the large garden. When their parents decided that the house must have additional wings to make it large enough for its purpose they had wonderful times climbing about on the scaffolding and 'helping' the workmen.

The Chief Guide's children were a never-ending joy to her and her diary in those days was used largely to record their stages in progress and their quaint childish remarks. It was only a stern sense of duty that took her so often from home in the service of that larger family of which she had, willy-nilly, become head.

No sooner had they settled into Pax Hill than the demand came for them to visit Canada and the United States. This meant a three months' absence from the little family. Even more heart-rending was the journey to India in 1921—necessary if the Movement were to be established on the right footing. Both parents and children suffered during these enforced separations.

However busy with Scouts and Guides when at home, the Chiefs usually managed to get back in time for nursery tea with the family on Sunday. During the long absences overseas this treat was much missed, as were the early-morning bedroom romps and the after-tea hour downstairs.

With the whole world their parish you might perhaps expect that the immediate neighbourhood, the village and parish circle, would be overlooked. But not only were there tea parties and garden parties for all and sundry, but also opportunities for local Scouts and Guides, Women's Institute, country dancers, and other village organizations, to meet at Pax Hill.

A day in the summer—or sometimes two—would be set aside for the Headquarters Staffs of the Scouts and Guides to desert their London offices and come down to spend a happy time having lunch and tea with the Chiefs. The ice-cream man would also be invited to the party with instructions to attend to all orders and send his bill to Pax later!

At the hub of all this never-ending activity was the Chief Guide.

'*I do love making plans*,' she would say, and if she had not been such a very good planner neither she nor the Chief Scout could possibly have done what they did. Of course, she had willing helpers—far too numerous to mention—but these had to be directed too.

If a Commissioner arrived to discuss problems, or a secretary came down from London to help with letters, these had to be met and fed and often housed.

THE WORLD OUR PARISH

The household staff must have their holidays and times off; the children must have their nurses and governesses, their clothes, doctors, dentists, and schools arranged.

As if three children were not enough, large-hearted Olave also took over the entire care of one of her sister's children (Auriol died in 1919), and the two other girls spent most of their holidays at Pax Hill in preference to their grandmother's London flat. So there were often six young children to feed and clothe and care for.

Now it seemed indeed that the Chief Guide was making up for the leisured life which she had led in those long carefree days before her marriage. She worked unceasingly, and few people will ever realize just how she did work in those days.

She wrote letters and chaired Conferences and Committees and inspected camps, and travelled the United Kingdom, organizing, planning, gathering in helpers, and often speaking at three or four meetings a day.

The great idea which lay behind much of her planning and work was to save her husband from any unnecessary labour or worry. She knew that he had more than enough to do without becoming involved in domestic or household problems. She was his constant protector from the inopportune or trouble-

some caller, shutting him away in his study if she felt
that the visit might be prolonged or prove an interruption to his thinking, and handing over whole
sheaves of papers from his desk, when he was not
looking, to his secretary to deal with.

Her first duty, as she now saw it, was to keep him
fit for his big job, fit in mind as well as in body, so
that he might be able to continue giving what he
alone could give to the Movement; and right thoroughly she performed this task.

When, years later, the Boy Scouts Association
decorated the Chief Guide with their highest award
of the Silver Wolf, it was largely in recognition of
her work in caring for their beloved Founder and
Chief. They realized what she had done and they were
grateful.

The award from the King in 1932 of the Grand
Cross of the British Empire proved that her work as
Chief Guide had not passed unnoticed by the world
at large.

# 9
# *The Pal-atelist*

SO PASSED the busy years—those last years of the between-wars peace; and what happy years they were for the Scout and Guide Movements and for the two Chiefs working hand in hand. Each day seemed to mark some step in progress, some landmark of which future generations of Scouts and Guides would speak as a jumping-off place to wider development.

Almost everything that has been proved to have been of vital importance to either branch was launched from Pax Hill, and for that reason alone the house—now in other hands—ought to come back one day to be for Scouts and Guides a place of pilgrimage. For those who knew Pax Hill the very walls speak of the Founder and of the Chief Guide.

For some years the Founder and his wife faced each other in the drawing-room where their two desks stood back to back by the windows. Then in 1924, the year of two big Jamborees and the first World Camp of the Guides, the first bricks were laid of the new wing which had been designed by the Chief for Pax Hill.

Each member of the family laid a brick. The new building included not only a large music room, with visitors' bedrooms overhead, but also a study for the Chief Scout where he could work in greater seclusion. Lady Baden-Powell continued to make the drawing-room her office, as she does today at Hampton Court Palace. Thus she was always accessible to visitors.

The thousands of Senior Guides—Rangers and Cadets—who converge each fifth year or so on London from every part of the country, to hold their meetings at the Albert Hall and to march proudly past their President, the Princess Royal, owe the name of 'Ranger' to a suggestion from the Founder at Pax Hill. The Chief Guide explained the reasons for this name in a note in the *Gazette* in June 1920.

'*Here is the suggested new name—Ranger. If you look it up in the Dictionary you will see that it means quite a number of things. "To range" is "to set in proper order", or "to roam", and this might well mean that you are going to tread ground as a Senior Guide which as a Guide you have not yet passed.*

' *"Distance of vision and extent of discourse or roaming power" again shows that as a senior member of the community you are expected to look further afield for good work which you can do for the community.*

' *"To range" means to travel, to rove over wide distances, whether your mind or your body.*

' *"A Ranger" is one who guards a large tract of forest or land, and thus can mean one who has the wide outlook and sense of responsible protective duties appropriate to a Senior Guide.*

' *Another definition is "to sail along in a parallel direction" and so we can feel that the Ranger Guides are complementary to the Rover Scouts.*

' *And so we hope that this new title will have the approval of all.*'

\*          \*          \*

In the same year—1920—the first World Scout Jamboree was held at Olympia, most of the plans for which emanated from the Founder's desk at Pax Hill.

The offer of a Guiders' Training House, Foxlease in the New Forest, was made by Mrs. Anne Archbold to the Chief Guide at Pax Hill in 1922; and then, while the Headquarters Committee were wondering whether they would ever be able to afford to run so large a place, Lady Baden-Powell received by telephone the news that Princess Mary (now the Princess Royal) would give the necessary money from her wedding presents to establish the place as Princess Mary House.

It was in the drawing-room at Pax, too, that plans for the original Guide International Committee and Overseas Committee took shape; and it was there that the World Association, that great international body which takes under its wing the Guides and Girl Scouts of the whole free world, came into existence.

The Chiefs had dozens of helpers and advisers in all these schemes; but the inspiration came from them in the first instance, and their co-workers and -planners spent days and nights at Pax Hill in order to have uninterrupted conferences with the heads of the Movement.

Walking round the grounds today, you can pin-point the spot where each new move originated. There is the lower drive where, at the end of 1918, the Chiefs had eaten their picnic lunch. Here, behind the house, is the cornfield where, sitting on a stook, the Chief Guide planned with Olivia Burges the first

World Camp. Where the big sofa and the square tea-table stood in the drawing-room you can still 'hear' the voices of Dame Katharine Furse and Mrs. Mark Kerr and others, planning out with the Chiefs the name to be given to the World Association.

And these are just a few of many dramatic moments. The whole house whispers them to you, and always the Chief Guide is there, in the middle of it all, not saying very much perhaps but listening intently to what the Founder and the others have to say.

By the time a new scheme had reached the Headquarters Committee for consideration it had usually been worked out to the last detail in the quiet surroundings of Pax Hill. And, taking shape there, rather than in the rush and hurry of a London office, such plans were often less formal and more suited to those for whom they were intended.

The play side of Guiding was always to the fore at Pax ('*If it's not fun it's not Guiding*', says the Chief Guide) and there were often living illustrations ready to hand on the lawn outside. Sometimes the children themselves would be roped in to play their part in making history. When the swimming pool at Fox-lease was opened by the Chief Guide in 1927 it was Heather—not her mother—who plunged in and had the first swim from end to end!

That all plans must be made for the benefit of the children, and not the children brought in to fill some framework devised by grown-ups, was an axiom with both the Chiefs, of which they were never tired of reminding their fellow-workers at Committees and World Conferences.

If it always seems to be summer, with camping and other outdoor occupations, when I write of Pax Hill, this is because it was usually the summers that the Chiefs spent in their home. During the coldest months they were often in India, Australia, South Africa, Canada, or the United States. Their presence in these places—and indeed in every country—was constantly demanded, and their visits were planned to take place if possible from January onwards when the English winter is usually at its unkindest and unsuitable for outdoor Scout and Guide Rallies.

The summer months were very full, with a year's work to be crowded into them, and the hospitality of Pax Hill so unbounded.

The summer of 1930 had been a particularly busy one and before the World Conference which was to be held at Foxlease there was a three-day meeting of the World Committee at Pax Hill.

'*A free day at home*', records the Chief Guide's diary for July 2nd, and it goes on to give some details of a 'free' day:

'*Fourteen Canadian Guiders come for picnic lunch and ten World Committee members arrive to stay. For tea we have also Guiders from Ceylon, Bermuda, the Gold Coast, and South Africa. Somehow we are managing to house all the World Committee members either in the house, the garden, the summer-house, the caravan, or, in two cases, with near neighbours.*'

After three busy days of talk the party left for Foxlease, where the delegates for the Sixth World Conference were assembling, and there, for the next ten days or so, the Chief Guide lived in the caravan, with the exception of a few brief intervals when she rushed back to Pax to attend to home duties.

'*It IS rather a relief*', she confided to her diary, '*to get home for a few quiet hours, as Foxlease, though delightful, is rather a whirl of talk.*'

But it was an important Conference for her, and one with far-reaching results for the Guides of the world.

On the pretext of a telephone call—a fictitious one —she was asked to leave the Conference and on her return she received the news that she had been unanimously chosen to be WORLD CHIEF GUIDE.

'*It is a huge honour*', she wrote, '*and I feel the responsibility very deeply.*'

And that is equally true today, though, without the Founder at her side to support and advise her, the responsibility weighs even more heavily.

May, June, and July were the busy months for Rallies, and in August there were always camps to be shared in or 'inspected'. September brought a little respite and sometimes a friendly sun when the family would go off on camping expeditions of their own, and the Chief Guide might even find a little time to garden and play tennis in the evenings.

Often they were at home right up until Christmas, when they were able to pick roses from the sheltered rose garden to decorate the table. The Founder loved roses, and the Chief Guide liked him to have them on his writing-table all the year round.

Christmas was a wonderful time for the children who grew up at Pax or spent their holidays there. For Lady Baden-Powell it began many weeks too soon because some two thousand Christmas cards had to be despatched from October onwards to Scout and Guide friends and workers in all parts of the world. The big list had to be brought up to date each year before the card, designed by the Chief and often containing the signatures of all the family, could be sent off.

*Extension Guides, though physically disabled, play their full part in the Movement. A Dutch Guide greets her Chief*

*With Nigerian Guides at Kano, 1957*

'Together.' For twenty years the two Chiefs worked hand in hand—and the world was their parish. Pax Hill, 1936

'Alone.' The Chief Guide carries on and the world is her parish. Hampton Court Palace, 1960

A few days before Christmas the Chief Scout would come down from his last meetings in London with his arms full of packages.

'I love parcel time, don't you?' the Chief Guide would say as she walked through the village on Christmas Eve, dropping gifts on various doorsteps, gifts always most carefully chosen.

Then there would be great expeditions for 'high-pulling' as the children called the collecting of holly and evergreens, and the house would be decked with these and with the hundreds of Christmas cards which came pouring in by every post.

Toy cupboards and bookshelves would be weeded out, and early on Christmas morning, before anyone was awake, 'Father Christmas' would steal down the drive and leave some parcels on the doorsteps of poorer neighbours with families of children.

After the great day, with its church and parcels and turkey and plum-pudding, would follow the parties and pantomimes, the 'thank-you' letter-writing, and about ten times as much work as usual for Lady Baden-Powell in acknowledging the cards and gifts, and noting the changes of addresses.

As each year drew to its end and they prepared for still more work and travel in the year to come, she need no longer record, as she had done in her girl-hood, that the months had been wasted!

Travel had always been a great hobby with the Founder, and he was delighted that his wife was such a splendid traveller. It suited them both that so much of their life together should necessarily be spent on board ship. Ever since their honeymoon in North Africa in 1913, and with the exception of some war years, they spent a good many weeks or months out of England in almost every year.

At the end of this book you will find a list of the countries which the Chief Guide has visited, first with the Founder and later by herself. But there is not much point in giving you this long list of names of places unless you can read into it something of the background which I have not space to describe.

First there was the time and work and expense and wear and tear involved in all this constant travel; but, far more important than that, there was the joy and wonder of the Scouts and Guides in these faraway places when their Chiefs came there for no other reason than to see—and to be seen by—THEM.

It must have been the high point in the life of many a Guide—as it still is today—when Lady Baden-Powell's uniform and her warm, welcoming, all-embracing smile appeared on the Rally ground, to which some of the children had often travelled many miles to meet her. It was not always even a Rally ground.

As they travelled long distances by train through the continent of Africa, through India or across Canada, there would be numbers and numbers of little isolated groups of Guides as well as Scouts at the small outposts where the train pulled up; and the Chief Guide, at whatever time of the day or night, would put on her uniform so that she might greet them correctly dressed as their Chief Guide.

Though the Chiefs enjoyed these long journeys, which were arranged as comfortably as possible for them by the host country, it was none the less an exhausting time, and they often felt amused when asked on their return to England: 'Did you have a nice holiday?'

Such parts of the 'holiday' not spent in talking with Scouts and Guides and their leaders, making speeches, and shaking innumerable left hands, were usually taken up with writing, or typing on 'Beetle', reports and letters and plans, while the train shook or the ship rolled or the plane bumped.

How often must Olave have felt on these occasions that it would be nice, even occasionally, to be free from work and responsibility, and to be able to do what she liked instead of having to like what she

did! But she never showed any signs of bore-
dom.

'*It was all very well worth while.*' That was how she
so often ended an entry in her diary describing some
particularly uncomfortable journey or some Rally
held in intense heat or in pouring rain, or perhaps a
visit to some very isolated spot just to see a few little
struggling Companies or Packs.

For her thought, first, last, and all the time, was—
and is—not for herself but for the Guides. Whether
it was half a dozen Guides at a railway halt or a Rally
of five or six thousand did not matter—it was the
individual Guide she cared about.

*          *          *

Up to 1930 she had travelled more or less unoffici-
ally in some countries, just to have a look at the
Guides while the Chief was seeing his Scouts; but in
1930 she was appointed WORLD CHIEF GUIDE by
the unanimous vote of all the countries which recognized Guides. This meant that henceforth her travels
must be governed by the needs of a particular country,
since the Movement abroad as well as in British
territory now came under her wing. This new title
put her on an equal footing with THE CHIEF SCOUT

OF THE WORLD—a title which her husband had held since 1920.

A 'world uniform', grey-blue in colour, soon took the place of her British Guide uniform in her travels abroad, and it is in this uniform that she is so well known today all over her Guide world.

It was on board ship that the Baden-Powells had first met—a foretaste of what their future lives together would be. It was a coincidence that Betty, their younger daughter, met her husband in the same way, and found out that—as in the case of her parents —they shared a birthday. (Peter, marrying in Rhodesia, had already made the same discovery about his wife Carine.)

As each journey came to an end, the Pax Hill postbag became heavier, and more and more names were added to the Christmas-card list.

Some people collect stamps; the Chief Guide collects friends! As with stamps, the older ones are often the more valuable—though she loves the bright new issues too!

Her collection now must be almost unique.

Now do you see why I headed this chapter *The Pal-atelist*?

But, while we are on the subject of stamp-collecting, you might be surprised to know that many postage stamps in recent years have borne portraits of the Founder and of Scouts and Guides. And in 1962 the Republic of Haiti produced a postage stamp with portraits both of the Founder and of the Chief Guide.

The Chief Guide has a large collection of such stamps in her scrapbooks. But I think she still values far more highly her collection of pals.

# 10

## *Home*

AND now, at the age of eighty, the Chief Scout was growing tired. Each summer brought yet more Scout Rallies, Jamborees, and Conferences, and more oversea Scouts to camp in Britain. Each winter brought its round of visits to Scouts about the world. And all this on top of endless office work, meetings, and the writing of books and making of speeches.

He was beginning, at last, to feel the strain of it all. The doctors said that he had a tired heart which would go on strike if he did not rest it.

What were they to do? It was quite impossible for the Chief to go on living in England and not to exert himself. It would have been like telling a cat to rest quietly among a roomful of mice.

He had always had a craving to go back to Africa to live for he had never quite got over his homesickness for the sunny land where he had spent so many good years of soldiering, sport, and Scouting.

Year by year the call grew louder and now it came, a summons to them both. Peter had joined the Rhodesian Police, was married, and the Chief's first grandson, another Robert Baden-Powell, had been born.

Betty had married a District Commissioner in Northern Rhodesia, and her daughter too had been born in Africa.

The difficulty was that all over South Africa and the Rhodesias were Boy Scouts, and the Chief could not see himself living there in the peaceful idleness which the doctors prescribed. He would certainly be drawn, willy-nilly, into active Scouting if he went there.

Farther north, in Kenya, the Baden-Powells had stayed during one of their long tours at a little place called Nyeri, where a friend who had once been on the Chief's staff was running a very successful hotel. It was in the grounds of this hotel, and within easy reach of its amenities—but outside the reach of Scouts —that they decided to build a little house to which he could retire quietly, away from all thoughts of work.

The house was to be called Paxtu, a word with an African ending which, as the Chief Guide said, could be taken to stand for Pax No. 2 or Pax for Two, or even Pax Too—a miniature edition of Pax Hill.

Not that it was going to be in the least like Pax Hill. It would be built on bungalow lines, without stairs, and with the minimum number of rooms.

The decision to build Paxtu was arrived at when, on a visit to Africa in 1938, the Chief had had some trouble with his heart and was unable to carry out a long programme of Scout engagements that had been prepared for him.

In 1937, after attending a wonderful World Jamboree in Holland, the Baden-Powells had celebrated their Silver Wedding. The Princess Royal attended the 'banquet' given to them by the Scout and Guide Movement, and handed over the beautiful gifts of silver plate for which both Headquarters had subscribed.

This occasion marked the climax of twenty-five years of happiness, a happiness which was shared by many thousands of young people everywhere.

So it seemed an appropriate moment to retire for a Silver Wedding honeymoon in the peace of their new home.

Heather was the only member of the B-P family to be left behind in England when at the end of 1938 the

Chiefs returned to Africa. But before their final departure they joined the good ship *Orduna*, which, with several hundred Scout and Guide people aboard, was cruising to Denmark, Iceland, Norway, and Belgium.

These Friendship Cruises had been instituted by the Chief Guide in a moment of inspiration. All her life she had wanted others to share in the good things which came her way. She considered it unfair that so many Guiders and Scouters, who were working hard with their Companies and Troops, never had the chance—as she had—of seeing 'how they did it' in other countries. So it was decided to book a whole ship, to fill it with Scout and Guide folk, and to visit brothers and sisters over the water. In the 1930s cruising was popular and there was not the slightest difficulty in finding enough people to fill the ship.

The first cruise, in 1933, was on board the *Calgaric* to the Northern Capitals of Europe—the Baltic countries where Scouting and Guiding were very much alive. This was so entirely successful and enjoyable that two further cruises were organized, one in the *Adriatic* in 1934 to the Mediterranean, calling at Gibraltar, Malta, Nice, Algiers, and Lisbon; and the third in 1938.

The enthusiasm aroused by these voyages was great,

both on board ship where the Scouters and Guiders were delighted to be sailing with the Chiefs and with one another, and at every port of call, where Scouts and Guides welcomed the party with open arms and carried them off to camp-fires and Rallies and feasts and on sight-seeing expeditions.

In return the local people paid visits to the ship and were entertained on board by the cruising party.

The Founder was allowed to go on this *Orduna* cruise, but forbidden by his doctors to take any active part in the proceedings, so the Chief Guide had to do a double share of handshaking and fraternizing.

The cruisers themselves were unanimous in their wish for further expeditions of the same kind, but the outbreak of war a year later put an end to such plans.

The Chiefs sailed from England for the last time together on October 27th, 1938, and after a peaceful voyage they arrived at Nyeri to find their beautiful brand-new home ready and waiting. They were quite delighted with everything, and on New Year's Day 1939 the Chief Guide wrote in her new diary:

'*A radiant and lovely dawn on a New Year in our dear wee Paxtu; the Mountain (Kenya) so beautiful and clear and all so calm and peaceful in this lovely spot.*

'*Walked down to early service in little Nyeri church, and met a whole lot of friends.*'

From that day onwards Lady Baden-Powell devoted herself entirely to the care of her loved invalid. She realized that their time together could not now be very long; and during the two years that followed they were seldom out of each other's sight.

At Easter Heather flew out to visit them, and then the family—including the grandchildren—came to Nyeri to see them. Betty's son, Robin, was born in Kenya on his parents' birthday, April 16th, 1939, and his grandfather was his first visitor.

The plan was to return to England for the summer of 1940 for a great family reunion at Pax Hill before finally retiring; but the outbreak of war in September 1939 knocked all such plans on the head, and in any case it is doubtful whether the Chief could have stood such a journey. But at least he had enjoyed looking forward to it.

He revelled in the life at Nyeri, and the go-as-you-please existence, though he was by no means idle. Some of his best water-colour sketches were done there, for now at last he had time to devote to them, and he wrote and illustrated three books and many magazine articles, as well as writing for his Scouts. But now he felt free to work or not as he pleased.

Time was no longer pressing and what he did not feel well enough to do today could be done tomorrow. How very different from the exacting itineraries of the past forty years and more!

When he felt well enough to fish, the Chief Guide drove him out to The Bend, eighteen miles away, which was a perfect fishing and picnicking spot; and when they felt like seeing a little more of life they just drove down to Nairobi, where shops and doctors and dentists and cinemas could be found.

While he was resting or reading or sketching, the Chief Guide sometimes played tennis and squash, and if she occasionally felt like a deserter, remembering all her previous activity, the feeling quickly went, for she knew that her duty was to stay with her husband for as long as he needed her.

She was certainly not idle. She wrote more articles for *The Guider* and *The Guide* than she had had time to do in her busy life; she 'did Brownies' with some small neighbours; and she took over the Commissionership of the Kenya Guides.

But her main job now—and her delight—was to be at the Chief's beck and call, to drive him round the countryside where he loved to 'stalk' wild animals with his cine-camera; to persuade him to eat when he was not hungry, to play chess with him, and to be wife, nurse, and secretary in one.

For two years they lived this life of quiet happiness and then—on January 8th, 1941—the inevitable parting came.

*        *        *

Scouts and Guides have a sign which they use when out tracking to signify to those who come after them that they have gone home. It is a dot within a circle, usually made with sticks or stones.

This sign marks the grave at Nyeri, at the foot of the mountain on which he loved to gaze, of one of the great men of the world.

He had gone home—and Olave was left to face the future without him. And the future seemed very dark.

When the hundreds of Memorial Services had been held, and the thousands of cables, telegrams, letters, and messages answered, life was indeed blank.

For over a year she stayed on in Africa, taking over the organization of the East African Women's League in addition to her work for the Guides.

The war had reached its worst stage, and it would have been much the easiest course to remain in sunny Kenya till it ended. But Olave was not looking for ease. Her conscience told her that there might be something she could still do, as Chief Guide, and this feeling was strengthened by letters from home saying that there was work for her which could be done by no one else.

Through a sea laced with mines, she returned to England in September 1942, took up the threads of war-time Guiding, and settled into a new home at Hampton Court Palace. Pax Hill was in the hands of the War Department and all the furniture in store.

It was a strange life for one coming from the peace and sunshine of Kenya. Most people at home had been acclimatized gradually to problems of black-out, rationing, lack of transport, and other amenities. To the Chief Guide all these restrictions came suddenly and they added greatly to the bleakness of life.

For two years she did a truly wonderful job in travelling round by whatever means were available to see and cheer the Guides at a time when such visits made an immense difference to morale and gave fresh impetus to people who were feeling the strain. Nothing was too much trouble, no journey too tiresome if it could be of use, and in carrying on the work which the Founder had left for her to do she herself gradually gained comfort and peace.

When the war at last came to an end the Chief Guide went at once to Paris. Scouting and Guiding had been forbidden in Occupied France, yet forty

thousand of these youngsters were there when she
took the Salute at a March Past. It took them nearly
two hours to march past the saluting base in files
twenty deep. And that was Paris alone! Wherever
the Chief Guide went on her tour of the country there
were groups, large or small, of Scoutisme Français
waiting to receive her.

It was the same in Belgium, in Luxembourg, in
Holland, Italy, and Norway. Whatever the difficulties, and however severe the suppression, this seems
only to have brought out the best and strongest
Scout and Guide spirit in anyone who had ever
belonged to the Movement.

That was in 1945; and each year since then has
seen more and more countries opening up Scouting
and Guiding to the masses of children for whom the
training is more than ever needed and by whom the
great game is more than ever welcomed.

*          *          *

It was the Founder who fired the spark that first
set Guiding alight, but the material was there all the
time, inflammable stuff, ready to burn when it got
the chance. It is the Chief Scouts who have followed
the Founder, and also the Chief Guide, with their

*'Thinking Day' swells the Chief Guide's post, which is always a large one, coming from all corners of the world*

*'Au revoir,' Jersey Guides*

*The World Chief Guide, 1962*

thousands of followers and helpers everywhere, who have been the breeze to fan the flame and keep the fire going and they have helped to spread it so widely that nothing can ever stop it—though here and there it may sometimes be damped down!

During the war firemen (dictators and others) thought they had stamped it out. What they had actually done was to drive it underground. As fire runs along underneath the bracken and starts up again in unexpected places, so beneath the surface the spirit of Scouting and Guiding was very much alive during nearly six years of hostilities. When peace came the Movement arose stronger and brighter than ever. Some of the formerly oppressed countries had doubled and even trebled their numbers during the years of stress and suppression.

Again, when the Chief Scout went to live in Kenya, as I have implied earlier, there were not many Scouts there to 'trouble' him. Now, since other 'troubles' have come to that country, when the Scouts and Guides had to carry out their work under great difficulties, the Movement there has spread and increased out of all recognition.

When a great Jamboree or Camp or Pageant is being mooted in any part of the world one of the first questions to be asked is 'Will the Chief Guide be there?' This is as true of Australia and New Zealand,

E

Norway and Holland, as it is of Oxford and Margate. The thought of her possible presence inspires all to make that particular show the best in the world.

If they have not met the Chief Guide before there may perhaps be a little shyness and formality at first, but the sunshine of her smile does away with all this and the whole atmosphere changes from that of an inspection to that of a party, where everyone feels friendly and at ease.

This is reminiscent of the Founder, her husband, who on arriving to inspect Scouts would sometimes shatter the more officially minded by observing to the boys: 'Well, you *have* got a lot of ugly faces!'

Prophets are said to be without honour in their own country and certainly one's family is usually the last to express admiration of one's efforts; so I must quote here what Betty, the Chief Guide's younger daughter, then aged seventeen, wrote about her mother. They had been travelling together round the Union of South Africa, where the various racial difficulties make themselves felt in Scouting and Guiding as in everything else.

'*Mum has been perfectly wonderful—she never seems tired and never gets bored or sick of people, and she does*

*speak well. I've heard practically every speech she's made
and I'm nowhere near tired of it yet.'*

As a speaker the Chief Guide usually makes no
special preparation and would never dream of having
a written address, unless of course it is a radio talk
where it must be submitted beforehand, or where it
has to be translated into another language. Normally
she prefers talking freely and intimately of things she
has done, people and places she has visited, Guides
she has met, and it is all very homely and friendly.
But her talk, though apparently haphazard, has always
its point and that point is usually concerned with
friendship through Guiding as one of the best contributions towards peace in the world.

She is the joyous bearer of messages of love and
friendship between Guides of different nations.

Of her visit to Greece in 1948 a Greek Guider wrote:

*'When, in 1930, the title of Chief Guide of the World
was conferred on Lady Baden-Powell by the World Conference in England, she said "I will do my best to help
everybody, everywhere." Ever since, this has been her one
great aim in life. It is the impression you get directly you
face her energetic countenance. Generally great expecta-
tions are never fulfilled. In this case Lady Baden-Powell's
personality proves irresistible; a smile full of kindness and*

*faith, two bright eager eyes, hands that instinctively "give the hand", a tireless vitality that is always ready, an indomitable wish to serve ... thus she was seen, greeted and loved by the Greek Girl Guides of Athens, Epirus, Macedonia.'*

It is the same wherever she goes. When, in 1955, she visited a town in Canada she received from the Brownies the totem name of SPARKLE, because, they explained, she had come there to fan the flames of Guiding.

'*Yes,*' said the Chief Guide, '*Spark is the word, but what about the last two letters, L and E?*'

'*They are the first and last letters of* LOVE *because we love you and we know that you love us,*' said they.

There I think is the secret of the Chief Guide and her success in fanning and getting others to help to fan the flame of this great world-wide Movement for good. She cares so much for each and every member of it, whoever and wherever they may be. The fact that they are fellow-Guides is quite enough to arouse her affection, and that is why they all want to come and meet her and talk to her and hear from her own lips how much she cares for everyone in this, her enormous family of children past and present—yes, and future too.

You may be a small newly joined Guide, Brownie,

Scout, or Cub, or you may be a V.I.P.—the Commissioner of a county or of an overseas colony, or
the Chief Guide of a foreign country. Your uniform
may be green or grey or brown or blue or white, and
your cheeks may be black or brown or rosy pink—it
does not matter. If you have made your Promise and
are carrying out your Law you are a special part of the
Chief Guide's special family, and her heart is large
enough to hold you all.

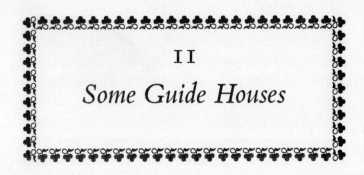

# 11

# *Some Guide Houses*

I HAVE told you in previous chapters about some of
the Chief Guide's perches—the homes from home
where a warm welcome and a warm bed will always
await her as she travels swiftly round the world on
visits to her scattered family.

These Guide Houses are the happy family meeting
places, as well as training schools for Guiders or Girl
Scout leaders and camping places for the Guides and
Girl Scouts.

In Great Britain Foxlease is one of the best-known
Guide Houses, and in 1962 Foxlease celebrated the
fortieth year of its existence as a Guide House. It was
one of the wettest days of a very wet summer, but
Guiders turned up in their hundreds to meet the Chief
Guide, to reminisce with one another, and to give
thanks to God for what Foxlease had given them.

Then there is Waddow in Lancashire, Our Ark in London, Lorne in Ulster, Netherurd in Scotland, Broneirion in Wales, to name just a few of the happy centres where Guiders congregate and Guides camp, and where the Chief Guide loves to call in for a night.

In France there are several of these Guide Houses—I have already told you about Les Courmettes in the south, and there is also Le Nef in Paris; and in Norway, Sweden, Denmark—every country in fact—there are such centres where the left hand of Guide fellowship will be held out to members of the Movement, no matter where they come from.

I want to tell you now about one of the best known of them all—and that is 'Our Chalet', 'Notre Chalet', or 'Unser Chalet', in Switzerland. Foxlease was given to the Guide Movement in Great Britain by an American, Mrs. Anne Archbold; and 'Our Chalet' was given to the Guides of the world by another American, Mrs. J. J. Storrow. I think it is fair to say that this wonderful gift was made because of Mrs. Storrow's love for, and admiration of, the Founder and the Chief Guide and their work.

This love and appreciation came about almost in spite of herself, because when in 1919 the two Chiefs were invited to go to America to see how the Movement was getting on there, Mrs. Storrow was not quite sure that she wanted them to come. She thought that perhaps they might want to lay down the law or try to anglicize the American Scout Movement, and she was a little bit apprehensive. She met them, perhaps prepared to receive them a little coldly; and she was completely bowled over by them both. They came, they saw, and they conquered. '*Something happened,*' said the Chief Guide, '*that wonderful something which makes us all friends in the twinkling of an eye when we find and blend the burning love of a common cause.*'

That may have had something to do with it certainly, but the personal charm and friendliness of the two Chiefs must have played a great part in disarming her. From that day forward 'Aunt Helen', as they called her, was a friend indeed to them both, and —because of them—a friend not only to American Scouting but to the whole world of Scouts and Guides.

The International Boy Scouts had already their Chalet at Kandersteg in Switzerland, at which the Scouts of all nations could meet to climb and camp and do winter sports together; and the Chief Guide remarked to Mrs. Storrow that she hoped that one day the Guides would be able to have theirs too.

No sooner said than done! Mrs. Storrow offered to give the Chalet, and this fairy godmother of a woman threw herself with all her energy into the

project, started out to find the right site for a chalet
and, when found, to supervise the building of it
among the lovely mountain slopes at Adelboden.
Beside it she also built a tiny chalet for herself so that
she could go there and enjoy the sight of her gift
being used; and it must have been the greatest joy to
her in her later years to see what infinite value her
gift was proving as a meeting place for the girls of all
nations.

Mrs. Storrow became the first Chairman of the
World Committee as well as carrying on her work
for her own Girl Scouts in America; but in Switzerland her name will always live, as well as in those
countries whose Guides have visited the Chalet and
seen her portrait hanging in the hall.

The Chief Guide is never happier than when she
can snatch a few days to spend in this, her Swiss home.
She goes there for Conferences and other work but
tries to slip in an extra day or two while there for
walking, climbing, ascending the mountain by air
lift, or just gazing at the view.

Here is her own description of a day at Adelboden:

*'The sun was just up and I looked out from my bedroom
window over the scattered roofs of the little houses of this
mountain village to the valley below.*

*'The high mountain peaks opposite were aglow with*

light and wreaths of mist were wafting away across the face
of the slopes opposite where I could just see the outline of
Our Chalet.

'The air was filled with the early morning noises of
country places. Cows were lowing near at hand in the dark
byres, cowbells were clanging far up the hillside pastures,
chickens squawked, hens cackled, the wheels of farm-carts
were creaking up the lane, and people were calling to one
another as the men went off to their farming and the women
were cleaning up their kitchens and outhouses and having
a bit of a chat to their neighbours as is the way of women all
the world over.

'It was all so peaceful, so homely, and so lovely. A
Guiders' Conference was going on and Commissioners
from all corners of the globe were gathered together to talk
over how best we could continue to further Guiding, and,
through it, how we could further friendship and goodwill in
the world.

'But I escaped from work that morning and went off
alone to walk up to the Chalet.

'It was piping hot and I strolled down the steep zigzag
path to the river and had a lovely time by the saw-mill
watching the piles of fresh cut logs sliding into the mill race,
and sniffing up the delicious scent of the fragrant pine
shavings lying under the saw benches.

'Those of you who have been to Our Chalet can picture
that turn in the road, and see again in your mind's eye the

*lovely mountain path that then winds up from the tossing river between mossy banks and lush flower-filled grass.*

*'There are sudden bends in the path, where you go under groups of overhanging fir trees which cast black shadows on the stony edges. And you just have to keep stopping to gaze away down the valley, bathed in blue sunlight and crowned by relays of snow-capped mountain peaks.*

*'I was standing drinking in this lovely scene when a group of some twenty Guides came running down the path towards me—hatless, bare legs, sun-tanned arms, gay, laughing, and carefree.*

*'Seeing that I was a Guide but not knowing in the least who I was, they stopped to talk.*

*' "What are you doing here?"*

*' "We are camping, up at Our Chalet."*

*' "Where are you off to now?"*

*' "We are going to learn to swim in the village swimming-bath."*

*' "What is happening up at the Chalet?"*

*' "There's lots going on. It's a grand place and we've made lots of friends."*

*' "Who is there now?"*

*' "Oh, Australia and Belgium and England—Surrey I think—and Finland and America and a Dane or two."*

*' "And who are you?"*

*' "We're Luxembourg—and who are you?"*

'*I felt quite embarrassed at having to explain myself to them as "what they call the Chief Guide".*'

That was before the Second World War, and how that day came back to the Chief Guide as, from her home in Kenya, she thought and hoped and prayed for the Guides in Luxembourg during the dark days which followed.

Yes, the Chief Guide feels that if America owes the idea of Scouting to Britain, Britain and the Guide world too owe more than they can ever repay to the generosity and wide-mindedness of individual Americans.

Another such enterprising American friend was Mrs. Juliette Low. On that fateful voyage in the *Arcadian* in 1912, when the Founder (a confirmed bachelor!) had met Olave Soames, there had been on board the same ship another passenger who was destined to play a big part in World Scouting. This was, of course, long before Olave had joined the Guides, but Mrs. Low had made friends with the Founder over their mutual interest in sculpture. She had seen some of his work in the Academy and, being a sculptor herself, was glad to meet him.

From sculpture they went on to Anglo-American friendship and then, naturally, talked about Scouts and Guides, and, as I have told you in an earlier chapter, it was she who carried the Movement for girls across the Atlantic. Mrs. Low's name will always be honoured as the Founder of the Girl Scouts of America. Her home in Savannah, Georgia, has become a Guide House like those others which I have described.

'*The girls took a lovely trip to visit the birthplace of American Scouting*', writes a correspondent.

'*We saw Juliette Low's home where she was born, the Low home where she started the first Troop in America, the Museum, the S.S. Juliette Low ship, which is the name of our Mariner Troop ship, stayed in Gordonstoun Park, saw the lovely gates which she designed and forged, and the cemetery where she is buried. We had a wonderful time seeing the many things in the Museum and felt that we knew a great deal more about the things which have made Scouting what it is today. From Savannah we went on to camp at Camp Juliette Low on top of Look-out Mount, which she started as a training camp for leaders. Needless to say, all the girls came back full of enthusiasm for the game of Scouting and I am sure they will pass it on to others.*'

There are numbers of other fine Girl Scout Houses and Camps throughout the United States, usually named after the person who gave them, or in whose memory they were given. One of these is Camp Edith Macy, the chief national training camp of Girl Scout leaders, about forty miles from New York City. Here are 265 acres of most lovely rocky wooded country, a sanctuary for wild birds and animals and a wonderful camp and training ground.

This place was opened in 1926, when the World Conference and Camp was held there. It had been given in memory of Mrs. Macy and the buildings had only just been begun, and the architect and builders thought they could not possibly be ready in time for such a Conference. It was Mrs. Low's idea to hold the Conference there and she was quite determined to do it.

'Wait another two years,' she was advised, but she replied: 'If you wait another two years I shan't be here and I want to be at the Conference.'

Only Mrs. Low and her doctors knew how ill she was and she would never have mentioned it had it not been for her great wish to have that Conference in her own country.

So everyone was stirred up to do their very utmost to get the place finished in time for the great event, and it was done—but only just.

*'It was as though we bowed the plasterers out of the back door while we welcomed our guests in at the front'*, wrote the Director.

The house was opened and dedicated at a special ceremony, attended by both the Founder and the Chief Guide, and the Conference of thirty-two countries took place there in the week that followed.

Mrs. Low had had her wish. She had welcomed the Guides of the world to America and she was satisfied. She died the following year, leaving as a legacy to her country this strong vigorous Movement for young America and an example to all Guides and Scouts of courage, energy, and devotion to the cause.

But she also left something tangible, which bears her name and by which she will be remembered not only in her own country but by Guides throughout the world.

The 'Juliette Lows' are groups of Guides and Girl Scouts from any and various countries who come together at 'Our Chalet' for a fortnight each summer to work and play and camp and cook together and to make friends and learn about each other's countries.

These girls are most carefully selected from amongst First Class Guides, 'Golden Eaglet' Girl Scouts, or whatever may be the equivalent in their own countries. They must have had at least three years' service and must have every intention of continuing to serve the Movement. They must have shown outstanding loyalty and keenness and Guide spirit and are, indeed, the final 'pick' of many fine specimens.

This free trip, usually extended to cover a good many European countries, is paid for by a World Friendship Fund which was instituted as a memorial to Mrs. Low.

How little she must have thought, when first meeting and talking to the Founder, that her name—like his—would live throughout the world in this way. How much better to have a happy and living memorial of this kind than a tablet or even a statue. Of her it might be written, as it was written of B-P himself:

*'Did any leave so many living monuments as you?'*

The Chief Guide is always especially glad to welcome a Juliette Low group to her home at Hampton Court, to hear of their friendships made, of their travels together, and of the wonderful Guide hospitality which they have received everywhere. The friendships made on such trips are cemented by letters, return visits, and reunions. In writing afterwards to the Chief Guide they usually refer to their visit to her home as one of the high-lights of a wonderful tour.

That Guiding is growing in numbers as well as in

quality would be evident, if we had not figures to
prove it, by the fact that almost every country has
outgrown its Headquarters. During the last few years
India, Canada, New Zealand, and many other countries and states as well as smaller centres, have had
to build; and fine new Headquarters buildings are
springing up every year.

The latest of the great World Guide Houses to be
opened is 'Our Cabaña' in Mexico. For a long time
the Guides and Girl Scouts in the Western Hemisphere had dreamed of a world meeting place on the
lines of 'Our Chalet' but a little nearer home. This
dream came true when, on Thinking Day 1956, 'Our
Cabaña' was dedicated in the presence of the World
Chief Guide. This lovely place, with its spacious
grounds and mountain views (did you ever at school
have to try to pronounce the name of Popocatepetl?)
is already becoming another home from home for
the Guides and Girl Scouts of the world. Tremendous
enthusiasm has gone into its building and its furnish-
ing in Mexican style, and the Chief Guide regards it
as her chief 'perch' in that part of the world, a world
that is growing smaller daily as facilities for encom-
passing it increase.

# 12

## *On the Wings of the Wind*

THE Chief Guide took to the air as a duck takes to water.

The Founder was not very fond of air travel, though on some occasions he had to do it, but his real love was for ships and the sea, and these necessary voyages gave him just the break that he needed between strenuous times of work.

Lady Baden-Powell loves ships and cruising too, but she also enjoys the speed of flight and, especially when she has long distances to cover, finds flying the most practical of all methods of travel.

It has certainly enabled her to see far more of her Guides than ever before. To be able to fulfil an engagement in England on Saturday afternoon and then to dash over to France or Germany, Denmark or

Iceland, for a couple of days, with hardly an interruption in her home routine, delights her, knowing as she does that if she is away too long her correspondence mounts up to an alarming extent.

For hopping round the continent of Africa where, in addition to her Guide contacts, she has a home and daughter and grandchildren, an aeroplane is the ideal answer.

The same is true of Australia, Canada, and the States, where distances are so vast and where a plane can enable her to visit Guides in spots out of reach of other transport. Flin-Flon for instance!

Flin-Flon is a flight of five hundred miles over 'nothingness' from Winnipeg in Manitoba. It is a town cut in rocks, discovered within the last few years to be rich in copper, gold, zinc, silver, cadmium, and selenium. Here, among hitherto silent forests and uncharted waters, there have suddenly sprung up mine and smelter buildings and with them civilization—including Scouts and Guides.

From Flin-Flon a 'Gold Cord' Guide represented the whole Commonwealth at the Coronation of Queen Elizabeth II in Westminster Abbey in 1953. When, later, the Chief Guide visited the place by air from Winnipeg, she had the joy of presenting six more Gold Cords to Guides there and yet another to a Guide who joined them from even farther north—

Churchill on the Hudson Bay. What a thrill for these Guides, and Scouts too, to see her in person. It was a red-letter day for them all.

The Chief Guide loves these small gatherings of scattered members of her flock just as much as the larger parades in the great towns and cities. To a Rally in the Rockies nine hundred Scouts and Guides arrived by a special train from Trail—another smelting plant town. Many of them had never been in a train before so they had a double dose of excitement.

Lady Baden-Powell has a wonderful memory for faces, due probably to her immense powers of observation. Even at a big Rally, where she sees hundreds of girls all dressed alike, she will often say to one: 'Have we met before?' and almost certainly the answer will be 'Yes—at the Swedish camp last year,' or 'Yes, I was at the Chalet when you came three years ago,' and so on.

On one occasion in Canada she was staying with a Guide President who told her that her daughter would be among the Guides at the Rally in the afternoon. The Chief Guide said at once: '*Do ask her to tell me, when I am inspecting her Company, who she is.*'

As she was walking down the lines at this huge Rally she was immensely amused to hear a small voice pipe out: '*I am my mother's daughter.*'

It delights her, on these oversea visits, to find so

many old friends. They may be Guiders whom she has seen as Guides at Rallies in Britain and who have gone overseas to work or to marry. Later they have come back to Guiding to hand on to the younger generation something of the good which they gained from it in their youth. This is constantly happening, and the fact that they have been through the mill and know the fun of Guiding (and also how to tie knots and signal) makes them all the more ready to lend a hand when asked to do so.

It is very nearly impossible for the Chief Guide now to talk to anyone in any country without finding that they have at some time had some sort of connection with the Movement. Even when she enters a shop, a hotel, or a plane, she is recognized and told when or where she was last seen—usually, if it is a man, at one of the World Jamborees.

In Northern Rhodesia not very long ago the Chief Guide was travelling by car through some of the wilder parts of the country and seeing little groups of Guides in the villages—a village consisting usually of a group of mud huts.

These children, whose 'uniform' consisted mainly of a badge, a tie on which to pin it, and a coloured head-band, were most enthusiastic Brownies and Guides, and their displays, particularly their lovely rhythmic singing and dancing, delighted their Chief. For the most part their dances were African ones but at one place she found they had learned the old English dance 'Galopede'.

Do you think she could resist joining in?

'*I think some of the Guides in England would have laughed to see me*', she wrote, '*on a wide dusty ground, in grilling sun, all of us cavorting about together with large grins on our faces.*'

The grin, to the Chief Guide, is one of the important parts of country dancing.

'*You needn't of course imitate the fixed smile of a film star, but if you are enjoying the dancing—as you should be —then it is much more fun for the onlookers, as well as for yourself, if you let your face slip, so to speak, and show your enjoyment on it. That's what it's there for!*'

That little Guide Rally must have been rather a different affair from some of the rest of the county, national, and international Rallies she attends and from events like the All-England Senior Branch Rally in London. Yet to their World Chief they are all just Guides and she is one with them, whatever they may be doing.

She is a very easy and adaptable person, always

most ready to do just what is wanted of her at a Rally or meeting; but she has just a few rules which she likes observed because they make things easier for everybody.

At a big Rally, or Church Parade, when the Colour Party and V.I.P.s enter in slow procession after the Guides or Scouts are in their places, she has suggested that a quiet signal to 'inward face' would enable everyone in the hall to see the procession and the incomers to see the faces, and not merely the backs, of those present.

(You know how, at weddings, the congregation longs to see the bridal procession enter the Church and those in front can only do so by casting guilty surreptitious glances over their shoulders. If they, too, 'inward faced' as an accepted part of the ceremony, everyone would be much happier—but that is a matter for the Churches!)

When seeing Guides, Lady B-P likes to be in uniform herself, and likes therefore to be warned beforehand and not to have surprise parties of them calling on her at home or popping up at railway stations when she is travelling privately. Whatever the Guides may feel about it, she feels uncomfortable if they are in uniform and she is not, just as a soldier going on parade would feel uncomfortable if he had not troubled to put on his uniform.

Occasionally it cannot be helped, and here is an amusing story of how she inspected Guides while wearing her night-gown.

It was in India when she was travelling with the Founder, and when the train stopped in the middle of the night at Baroda they were both fast asleep. But, without warning, a Guard of Honour of Scouts and Guides had hopefully turned out on the platform. The Chief Scout slipped on his shorts, shirt, and Scout hat quite quickly; but Guide uniform is a lengthier process and the Chief Guide knew it was no use attempting it. So, bundling her long hair under her Guide hat, she buttoned her Guide overcoat to the chin and inspected the Guides from the window of the carriage, and was just able to shake each by the hand—without revealing her feet—before the train moved off. For once she had been caught napping!

Talking about India, I came across this programme of what the Chief Guide had to do on one day during that same tour—and it will give you some idea of what is expected of her, though to that sort of programme today are added the radio and television interviews as well.

10 a.m.      *Meeting of Commissioners.*

11.30        *Meeting of members of Local Council and Associations.*

| 1.30 p.m. | *Lunch party.* |
| 2.30 | *Supposed to be 'rest hour' but letters had to be written.* |
| 4.0 | *Reception at Scout Headquarters with swimming display and presentations.* |
| 5.0 | *Guiders' tea party—shook hands with all the 150.* |
| 6.0 | *Visited Scouts at Clubhouse.* |
| 8.30 | *Dinner party.* |
| 10.0 | *Guide Ball for raising funds.* |

But we were discussing uniform; and this is what the Chief Guide says about it:

*'I feel most uncomfortable if I am caught unawares by a party of Guides waiting to be inspected and I am, as I consider, wrongly dressed. I feel in such cases that they will look at me and think to themselves: "She is only an ordinary person after all, and not one of us"—and so I become self-conscious and unhappy and feel out of it through not being dressed in the same uniform as those who are kindly waiting to bid me welcome. This does not often happen, I am glad to say, because I am proud of my uniform and like to wear it if there is any chance that Guides in uniform may be waiting to see me. I hope you all take a real pride in your uniform too—indeed I am sure you do!'*

The World Chief Guide, as I told you in the earlier pages of this book, has never been able to take an interest in fashion or to spend a lot of her time, as so many people do, studying clothes in shop windows or trying on dresses. She is just not made that way. She buys very few clothes and looks after them carefully so that they last a long time.

But she loves her uniform and as she wears it so often she is able to travel light, which in aeroplanes is very necessary.

Another of her rules—or requests—is that she should not be given bouquets when attending Guide Rallies. She thinks bunches of flowers are out of place with uniform and should not be carried.

And the same applies to presents. The reason for this should not be too difficult to understand. She cannot accept presents from everybody. If some give presents others may think it is 'the thing' to do, and follow suit, and the gifts would snowball out of all proportion. To those who do not know this, and bring offerings, the Chief Guide usually asks if she may hand them on to one or other of the Guide Houses or Headquarters, where they may be seen and admired, or used, as the case may be.

There are exceptions, of course, to every rule, and one such notable exception was the 'Ice Cream'. After the Chief Guide's recent visit to Australia the

Guides in one State decided that, to show their affection for their Chief, they would each buy her an ice cream. In other words, the very next time each one of them spent a few pence on an ice cream for herself, she would send an equal amount to the 'Ice Cream Fund' at Headquarters. With such numbers and enthusiasm it did not take very long for the pence to grow into thousands of shillings and thence into some hundreds of pounds; and just as the Chief Guide was going off on a long tour in the South American countries she was greatly surprised and touched at receiving quite a large ice-cream cheque to be spent on anything that she wanted.

There was one thing that she wanted very badly. In some of the Spanish- and Portuguese-speaking countries of Central and South America the Guides were having a hard struggle to get enough literature in their own languages to enable them to carry on the Movement. Their development was being seriously hampered through lack of the right books. So on her return to England the Chief Guide arranged for quantities of these to be sent as free gifts not, as she said, from herself but from their sister Guides in Australia. I can't tell you, because I don't know, how many Guides in the Western Hemisphere received help from this fund, but I know there must have been hundreds of them, and that the whole of this

generous gift went to forwarding the Movement in
one way or another. Even the garden seats for her
roof-garden, the few things which she bought for
herself, were really needed only that she might give
better hospitality to her visiting Guides.

Once when the Scouts of the world wanted to give
a penny each towards a present for the Founder, his
wife was commissioned to ask him what he most
wanted—to which he replied that the only thing he
really needed was a new pair of braces! These were
duly presented to him, along with a Rolls-Royce and
trailer caravan. The Founder believed, and taught,
that the happiest person was not the person with the
most money but the person with the fewest needs—
and he reckoned that he had none.

So with the Chief Guide. When asked what she
most wanted she replied: '*A piano for "Our Cabaña"* '
—and so right across the Atlantic and down to Mexico
went little contributions of money from many Guides
and friends, towards the cost of the piano which was
to benefit so many members of her family when
visiting their Mexican Guide Home.

No flowers—no presents—and she has one other
little stipulation and that applies to the signing of
autographs.

Autograph hunting is infectious and if one Guide,
at a Rally, thinks it would be nice to get the Chief

Guide's signature and comes along with her book, she is usually followed by dozens of others who think: 'Well, if she can get it, why shouldn't I—even if I don't especially want it?' Then the Chief Guide is forced to say 'No' and she dislikes that very much indeed. So she always hopes that the Guides will be content with seeing her and being seen by her and will not demand her autograph as well. In any case it is not easy, when carrying out a programme to time, to fit in extras like that.

Autograph collecting is not a 'Scouty' or 'Guidey' hobby, because it demands no effort on the part of the collector and gives trouble to others. Whereas a collection of wild flowers, stamps, flint implements, shells, or something of that sort, can be both absorbing and educative.

★ ★ ★

Apart from these small matters, no Guide can ever enjoy a Rally more than the Chief Guide does. She shows her interest, pleasure, and enjoyment at every turn and always tries to make the affair as informal and easy as possible; telling the Guides to move round and 'shake' themselves when they have been standing for some time; and getting them to sit close beside her on the ground or on anything that is handy, when she is yarning to them. Or she will tell them that Guiding has received so many pats on the back that she would like each Guide to pat her neighbour on the back, because it is *they* who have made Guiding what it is. And that makes a lot of fun.

In the United States, where on one tour she gave 158 talks to Girl Scouts and their leaders, she never showed the least sign of being tired or hurried, and the letters which followed her after each occasion showed that she had given, as well as gained, inspiration and encouragement.

*'I love that country and so many people in it'*, she writes. *'It needs to be far better known and understood on this side of the Atlantic, for behind and beyond the façade of newspaper publicity regarding its trials and tribulations lies a nation of vigorous, forceful, splendid people living grand sound lives, making fine good homes, and with hearts that are generous and kind to the umpteenth degree. Never have I felt greater warmth of welcome anywhere, and the eagerness with which one is made to feel at home is most touching and heart-warming. I have been thrilled anew by all that I have seen and felt and heard of Scouting over there and only wish that every one of you could have shared some of the experiences with me that have been so stimulating and encouraging.'*

The love is certainly not all on one side.

'*I feel kinda special every time I get a letter from you*', wrote one Girl Scout leader; and another from a town in California:

'*Your ability and charm seem to be inexhaustible to say the least; what a wonderful life yours is.*'

And the American wife of the Military Attaché in a European capital wrote in 1962 to the author of this book:

'*Just to think of her is to be encouraged and stimulated to be a better person for having thought of her. She is one of the great people of the world today, not just well known but truly GREAT in the highest sense of the word.*'

Hundreds of letters like that are in the post as the years go by. She has surely enshrined herself firmly in the hearts of Americans, young and old, and by letters and return visits when they come to England the friendships are kept alive.

In 1955 the Chief Guide paid her tenth visit to America and Canada, during which time she travelled 18,409 miles by car—right across Canada and down the western seaboard of America, then back to

New York; as well as 3,000 miles by air and 400 by
train. She made a total of 290 speeches, apart from the
many other functions—and never missed an appoint-
ment, or failed through illness or any other reason to
carry out her programme.

A pretty wonderful record, don't you think?

With the year 1957 came not only the Centenary
of the Founder's birth, but also the Golden Jubilee of
the Boy Scout Movement—founded in 1907. A great
service of thanksgiving in Westminster Abbey on
February 22nd started the year of celebrations which
culminated in a World Jamboree at Sutton Park in
Warwickshire and a World Camp of Guides in
Windsor Great Park. These events, attended by the
Queen and the Duke of Edinburgh, by the Princess
Royal and the Duke of Gloucester, were world news,
and one person who was indispensable at each and
every gathering was of course Olave Baden-Powell.
A time for her of poignant memories as well as of joy
and thanksgiving, she was in constant demand for
speeches, for messages, for Press, television, and radio
interviews, as well as an unusual number of visitors
including every member of her personal family to
share in the rejoicings.

Since that date no year has passed when in one
country or another the Scouts have not been celebrat-
ing their Golden Jubilee; and in 1960 came the turn

of the Girl Guides in Britain and in Canada, followed closely by numbers of other countries.

So that, far from spending her later years in peace and retirement, the Chief Guide is now busy sharing Jubilee Camps and Rallies in many of the countries which so quickly followed Britain's lead in starting their Guide movements.

*     *     *

Most of the jobs which people do in life are those which others have done before them, so that the duties pertaining to them have been laid down either by rule or tradition or both. Thus, if you wish to become a hairdresser, a nurse, or a cook, there is not very much doubt about what will be expected of you, though details may vary.

But the duties of a WORLD CHIEF GUIDE have never been laid down, because Olave Baden-Powell is the only one of her kind; so she has had to decide for herself how and where she can best carry them out.

Her view is that she ought to see and know as many as possible of her large family, in as many places as possible; and that the only way to do this is to travel a great deal, to speak over the air to those that she cannot visit; and to have a very large correspondence indeed.

F

Travel of course is the most important because it is the personal touch that she believes in so firmly; and that is why the Chief Guide must be one of the most travelled people in the world today.

Not only that but, through her example and enthusiasm, many other Scout and Guide people have travelled more widely than they would otherwise have done.

It was her inspiration which started the Friendship Cruises in the years between the wars, cruises which caused many stay-at-homes to visit other countries for the first time; and through camping and World Scout and Guide Houses thousands of young people have had the chance to do the same.

In 1962 the Chief Guide paid her first visit to Japan to see her 'children' there.

The Founder used to tell a story of a dream that he had, wherein he reached the gates of Heaven, but was stopped by St. Peter who asked him: 'And what did you think of Japan?'

'Japan? I never went there.'

'Never went to Japan? Why do you think God put you into a world of wonder and beauty if He meant you to stay in one corner all the time? Go back and see something of the world before you return here.'

So the Founder and the Chief Guide travelled—not so much perhaps to see the world, though they revelled in that too, as to see their Scouts and Guides.

That whole-hearted devotion which, as a little girl, Olave gave to her individual doves and chickens and dogs and rabbits, she now extends to each member of her husbands great Movement.

And what of her own personal family—the three children who lived with their father and mother at Pax Hill and grew up with the Scout and Guide Movement?

They all married and had families of their own.

Peter, the second Lord Baden-Powell, married Carine Boardman. Peter died in 1962 and their son, Robert, the Chief Guide's oldest grand-child, is the present Lord Baden-Powell. He married Patience Batty. Peter's other son, Michael, married Joan Berryman and their son, David Robert, is said to look very like his great-grandfather. Peter's daughter, Wendy, like her brothers and their wives, is a keen worker in the Movement that her grandfather started.

Heather married John King of the R.A.F. and had two sons, Michael and Timothy, who were both Scouts. The former lost his life in a tragedy at sea, while helping a non-swimmer on to a raft.

Betty married Gervas Clay, lately Director of the Rhodes Livingstone Museum. This couple play a great part in the Scout and Guide Movement as do their daughter Gillian (now Mrs. William Clay), and their sons Robin, Nigel and Crispin. Nigel married Elaine Hughes and he and Gill, as well as Michael Baden-Powell, have children of their own.

So the generations build up and it seems a far cry from the child of Chesterfield to the World Chief Guide with her children, grandchildren, and the great grandchildren now coming along—as well as her millions of Scout and Guide children.

May every one of these be a credit to her and to the Founder by doing his or her best to live up always to the Promise and Law.

# *Some Events in the Life of the World Chief Guide and her Travels*

1889  Born at Chesterfield, Derbyshire, England.

1903  Visited Scotland for two months.

1909  Visited Norwegian Fjords.

1910  Visited French Riviera.

1912  Cruise to the West Indies. Engaged and married.

1913  Gibraltar, Malta, Algeria, Italy.

1914  Scotland.

1915–16  France—serving in Army Recreation Hut.

1916  Appointed Chief Commissioner, Girl Guides.

1917  Appointed Chief Guide.

1918  France—visiting W.A.A.C.

1919  Tour in U.S.A.
Cologne and Belgian battlefields.

1920  First World Scout Jamboree, England.

1921  India, Burma, Ceylon, Palestine, Egypt.

1922  France, Switzerland.

1923  Canada, U.S.A.

1924  First World Camp, Foxlease, England.
      Denmark, Sweden.

1926  U.S.A. for World Conference.
      South Africa, Southern Rhodesia.

1927  South Africa, Sweden.

1928  Hungary for World Conference.
      Austria, Germany.
      Wales.

1929  Canary Is., Sierra Leone, Dakar, Tangier, Lisbon.

1930  West Indies, Panama, Cuba, Bermuda, U.S.A.
      Elected World Chief Guide at World Conference,
      Foxlease, England.

1931  New Zealand, Australia, South Africa.

1932  Switzerland, Poland.
      Awarded G.B.E.

1933  Malta, Italy, Gibraltar, European Northern Capitals.

1934  Gibraltar, France, Malta, Algiers, Portugal.

1935  Australia, New Zealand, Canada, Newfoundland,
      U.S.A., Kenya, Uganda, Tanganyika, Zanzibar.

1936  Northern and Southern Rhodesia, St. Helena, Sweden,
      France.

1937  India, Malta, Holland, Kenya.

1938  Northern and Southern Rhodesia, Kenya, South Africa, Switzerland.

1939–40  Kenya.

1941  Founder's death.
      Kenya, Tanganyika, Northern Rhodesia, Uganda, Belgian Congo.

1942  South Africa.

1943  England, Scotland, Wales, Ulster.

1944  English Counties, Isle of Man.

1945  France, Switzerland, Italy, Luxembourg, Belgium, Sweden, Norway, Denmark, Liechtenstein.

1946  Cuba, Mexico, West Indies, British Guiana, U.S.A., Canada, Newfoundland, France, Switzerland, Czechoslovakia, Holland, Eire.

1947  France, Australia.

1948  Australia, New Zealand, Panama, Curaçao, U.S.A., Greece, Malta, Italy, France.

1949  Wales, Scotland, Ulster, Switzerland, Sweden, Norway, Holland, Belgium, Denmark, Greece, Egypt, Sudan, Kenya.

1950  Kenya, Uganda, Tanganyika, Zanzibar, Northern and Southern Rhodesia, Nyasaland, Swaziland, Basutoland, South Africa, Belgian Congo, Nigeria, Gold Coast, Sierra Leone, Gambia.

1951 Guadeloupe, Martinique, Barbados, Trinidad, Tobago, British Guiana, Grenada, St. Vincent, St. Lucia, Dominica, Montserrat, Antigua, St. Kitts, Bermuda, Bahamas, Haiti, Puerto Rico.
Belgium for World Committee.

1952 Lecture tour in U.S.A. (45 towns).
Canada, Scotland, Norway, Switzerland.

1953 France, Canada, U.S.A.

1954 U.S.A., Bermuda, France, Sweden, Switzerland, Holland.

1955 Ulster, Isle of Man, Switzerland, Sweden, Canada, U.S.A.

1956 U.S.A., Mexico, Scotland, Germany, Iceland, Switzerland, Malta, Sudan, Uganda, Kenya, Northern and Southern Rhodesia.

1957 Kenya, Tanganyika, Zanzibar.
England for Centenary and Jubilee celebrations.
Ghana, Scotland, Denmark, Switzerland.
Australia.

1958 Papua, New Guinea, Fiji, Philippines, Hong Kong, Malaya, North Borneo, Sarawak, Ceylon.
Switzerland, Belgium, North Wales.

1959 Kenya, Scotland, Ulster, Brazil, Uruguay, Argentina, Chile, Peru, Ecuador, Colombia, Panama, Costa Rica, Nicaragua, El Salvador, Guatemala, British Honduras, Mexico.
U.S.A., Ireland.

1960 Gibraltar, Portugal, Germany, Denmark, Greece, Finland, Switzerland, Nigeria, Lebanon, Pakistan.

1961 India, East Pakistan, Burma, Ceylon, Italy, Isle of Wight, Canada, U.S.A.

1962 U.S.A., Canada, Denmark, Holland, Iceland, Switzerland, Sweden, Scotland ,Wales.
Japan, Korea, Hong Kong, Malaya, Kenya.

1963 Kenya, Thailand, Uganda, Tanganyika, Northern and Southern Rhodesia, Denmark, Greece.

1964 U.S.A., Mexico, Jamaica, Curaçao, Venezuela, Surina, Cayenne, Georgetown, West Indies, Kenya.

1965 Uganda, Sudan, Egypt, Scilly Isles, Luxembourg, Norway, Sweden, Canada.

1966 U.S.A., Mexico, Panama, El Salvador, Guatemala, Tokyo, Korea, Hong Kong, Thailand, India.

1967 U.S.A., Canada, Malta, Rome, Mexico, New Zealand, Australia.

1968 Kenya, Ceylon, India, Switzerland, Liechtenstein.

1969 Kenya, Finland, U.S.A., Canada, Finland, Nigeria, Channel Islands, Belgium.

1970 Kenya, South Africa, U.S.A., Denmark.

# Index